Making Collaboration Work

ManageMentor Skill Pack

MANAGE ■ MENTOR

BUSINESS MANAGEMENT

Lesson From,

Herminia Ibarra, Morten Hansen, Jeff Weiss,
Jonathan Hughes, Lynda Gratton, Tamara
Erickson, Bob Frisch, Amy Edmondson, Robert
Huckman, Bradley Staats, John Neffinger, Keith
Ferrazzi

Copyright © 2015 ManageMentor Business Management.
Nürnberg, Germany.

A CIP catalogue record for this title is available from the British
Library
ISBN: 1515007839

ISBN-13: 978-1515007838

Printed and bound by
Amazon Media EU S.à r.l. , 5 Rue Plaetis, L-2338 Luxemburg.

Amazon.com, Inc.; Seattle, WA 98108-1226, USA

CONTENTS

ACKNOWLEDGMENTS

- Herminia Ibarra is a professor of organizational behavior and the Cora Chaired Professor of Leadership and Learning at Insead. She is the author of *Working Identity: Unconventional Strategies for Reinventing Your Career* (Harvard Business Review Press, 2003).

- Morten T. Hansen is a professor at the University of California, Berkeley, and at INSEAD. He is the author of *Collaboration* and co-author of *Great by Choice*. In 2013, he was named one of the top management thinkers in the world by the Thinkers50.

- Jeff Weiss is an adjunct professor at the U.S. Military Academy at West Point and a partner at Vantage Partners, a Boston-based consultancy specializing in corporate negotiations and relationship management, where he focuses on sales negotiations and strategic alliances.

- Jonathan Hughes is a partner at Vantage Partners, specializing in supply chain management, strategic alliances, and change management.

- Lynda Gratton is Professor of Management Practice at London Business School where she directs the program 'Human Resource Strategy in Transforming Companies. Her most recent book is *The Shift: The Future of Work is Already Here*.

- Tamara J. Erickson is the author of a trilogy of books on generations in the workforce and has written several articles for HBR, including "It's Time to Retire Retirement" (March 2004), which won a McKinsey Award. A member of the Boomer generation, she is based in Boston.

- Bob Frisch is the managing partner of the Strategic Offsites Group, and the author of *Who's In the Room? How Great Leaders Structure and Manage the Teams Around Them* (Jossey-Bass/Wiley 2012). His most recent Harvard Business Review article was "Who *Really* Makes the Big Decisions in Your Company."

- Amy C. Edmondson is the Novartis Professor of Leadership and Management at Harvard Business School and author of *Teaming: How Organizations Learn, Innovate, and Compete in the Knowledge Economy* (Jossey-Bass, 2012).

- Robert Huckman is a professor at Harvard Business School.

- Bradley Staats is an associate professor at the University of North Carolina.

- Christine Congdon is the director of global research communications and Catherine Gall is director of workspace futures at Steelcase.

- Jeanne Brett is the DeWitt W. Buchanan, Jr. Distinguished Professor of Dispute Resolution and Organizations at the Kellogg School of Management, Northwestern University.

- Kristin Behfar, an associate professor at the Darden School of Business, University of Virginia, studies culture and team decision processes.

- Mary C. Kern is an assistant professor at the Zicklin School of Business at Baruch College in New York.

- Amy J.C. Cuddy is an associate professor of business administration at Harvard Business School. Matthew Kohut and John Neffinger are the authors of *Compelling*

People: The Hidden Qualities That Make Us Influential (Hudson Street Press, August 2013) and principals at KNP Communications.

- John Neffinger are the authors of *Compelling People: The Hidden Qualities That Make Us Influential* (Hudson Street Press, August 2013) and principals at KNP Communications.

CHAPTER 1
Are You a Collaborative Leader?

Social media and technologies have put connectivity on steroids and made collaboration more integral to business than ever. But without the right leadership, collaboration can go astray. Employees who try to collaborate on everything may wind up stuck in endless meetings, struggling to reach agreement. On the other side of the coin, executives who came of age during the heyday of "command and control" management can have trouble adjusting their style to fit the new realities.

In their research on top-performing CEOs, Insead professors Ibarra and Hansen have examined what it takes to be a collaborative leader. They've found that it requires connecting people and ideas outside an organization to those inside it, leveraging diverse talent, modeling collaborative behavior at the top, and showing a strong hand to keep teams from getting mired in debate. In this article, they describe tactics that executives from Akamai, GE, Reckitt Benckiser, and other firms use in those four areas and how they foster high-performance collaborative cultures in their organizations.

Watching his employees use a new social technology, Marc Benioff, the CEO of Salesforce.com, had an epiphany. His company had developed Chatter, a Facebook inspired application for companies that allows users to keep track of their colleagues and customers and share information and ideas. The employees had been trying it out internally, not just within their own work groups but across the entire organization. As Benioff read the Chatter posts, he realized that many of the people who had critical customer knowledge and were adding the most value were not even known to the management team.

The view into top management from the rank and file was just as obscure, Benioff knew. For instance, the company's annual management off-site was coming up, and he could tell from talking to employees that they wondered about what went on behind closed doors at that gathering. "They imagined we were dressing up in robes and chanting," he says.

What could he do to bring the top tier of the company closer to the workforce? Benioff asked himself. And then it hit him: Let's use Chatter to blow open the doors of the management off-site.

What greeted the 200 executives who attended that meeting was atypical. All 5,000 Salesforce.com employees had been invited to join them—virtually. Huge TV monitors placed throughout the meeting room displayed the special Chatter forum set up for the off-site. Every manager received an iPod Touch, and every table had an iPad, which attendees could use to post to the forum. A video service broadcast the meeting in real time to all employees, who could beam in and instantaneously express their views on Chatter, too.

The meeting began with the standard presentations. The managers watching them weren't quite sure what to do. Nothing unusual happened at first. Finally, Benioff grabbed the iPad on his table and made a comment on Chatter, noting what he found interesting about what was being said and adding a joke to spice it up. Some in the room followed with a few comments, and then employees watching from their offices launched a few comments back. The snowball started rolling. "Suddenly, the meeting went from a select group participating to the entire company participating," Benioff says.

Comments flew. "We felt the empowerment in the room," recalls Steve Gillmor, the head of technical media strategy.

In the end the dialogue lasted for weeks beyond the actual meeting. More important, by fostering a discussion across the entire organization, Benioff has been able to better align the whole workforce around its mission. The event served as a catalyst for the creation of a more open and empowered culture at the company.

Like Salesforce.com's managers and employees, businesspeople today are working more collaboratively than ever before, not just inside companies but also with suppliers, customers, governments, and universities. Global virtual teams are the norm, not the exception. Facebook, Twitter, LinkedIn, videoconferencing, and a host of other technologies have put connectivity on steroids and enabled new forms of collaboration that would have been impossible a short while ago.

Many executives realize that they need a new playbook for this hyperconnected environment. Those who climbed the corporate ladder in silos while using a "command and control" style can have a difficult time adjusting to the new realities. Conversely, managers who try to lead by consensus can quickly see decision making and execution grind to a halt. Crafting the right leadership style isn't easy.

As part of our research on top-performing CEOs, we've examined what it means to be a collaborative leader. We've discovered that it requires strong skills in four areas: playing the role of connector, attracting diverse talent, modeling collaboration at the top, and showing a strong hand to keep teams from getting mired in debate. The good news is, our research also suggests that these skills can be learned and can help executives generate exceptional long-term performance.

Taking Your Collaborative Pulse

1. **Play Global Connector**

   - Do you attend conferences outside your professional specialty?

   - Are you part of a global network like Young Presidents' Organization?

   - Do you regularly blog or e-mail employees about trends, ideas, and people you encounter outside your organization?

   - How often do you meet with parties outside your company (competitors, consumers, government officials, university contacts, and so on) who are not directly relevant to your immediate job demands or current operations?

   - Are you on the board of any outside organizations?

2. **Engage Talent at the Periphery**

   - How diverse is your immediate team in terms of nationality? Gender? Age?

   - How much time do you spend outside your home country?

   - Have you visited your emerging markets this year?

   - Does your network include people in their twenties (who aren't your kids)?

3. **Collaborate at the Top First**

   - Do members of your team have any joint responsibilities beyond their individual goals?

   - Does the compensation of your direct reports depend on any collective goals or reflect any collective responsibilities?

   - What specifically have you done to eradicate power struggles within your team?

   - Do your direct reports have both performance and learning goals?

4. **Show a Strong Hand**

   - Have you killed any collaboration projects in the past six months?

- Do you manage dynamically—forming and disbanding teams quickly as opportunities arise?
- Do the right people in your organization know they can "close" a discussion and make a decision?
- Does your team debate ideas vigorously but then unite behind decisions made?

5. Play Global Connector

In his best-selling book *The Tipping Point,* Malcolm Gladwell used the term "connector" to describe individuals who have many ties to different social worlds. It's not the number of people they know that makes connectors significant, however; it's their ability to link people, ideas, and resources that wouldn't normally bump into one another. In business, connectors are critical facilitators of collaboration.

For David Kenny, the president of Akamai Technologies, being a connector is one of the most important ways he adds value. He spends much of his time traveling around the world to meet with employees, partners, and customers. "I spend time with media owners to hear what they think about digital platforms, Facebook, and new pricing models, and with Microsoft leaders to get their views on cloud computing," he says. "I'm interested in hearing how our clients feel about macroeconomic issues, the G20, and how debt will affect future generations." These conversations lead to new strategic insights and relationships, and help Akamai develop critical external partnerships.

Connecting the world outside to people inside the company is crucial to Kenny. He uses a number of tactics to do this. "First, I check in on Foursquare often and post my location to Facebook and Twitter," he says. "It lets employees in different Akamai locations know I'm in town so that anybody at any level can bring me suggestions or concerns. Second, every time I go to one of our locations, I have lunch or coffee with 20 to 40 people. We go around the room, and people ask questions on topics they most want to address. Often my answer is to connect them with others in Akamai or even people at other companies who have expertise on the topic. Third, if I see a big opportunity when meeting with a customer or colleague, I will schedule a follow-up visit and bring along the right experts from Akamai. Fourth, whenever I travel, I try to make room to meet with two to three people I know in that location. Whenever possible, I bring someone else from Akamai with me to those meetings."

Kenny's networking recently resulted in an important strategic alliance with Ericsson. Akamai is now working with the mobile giant to change consumers' internet experiences on mobile devices. The partnership evolved out of a conversation Kenny had with a midlevel Ericsson executive two years ago at the Monaco Media Forum. "It really changed my idea of what Ericsson could be, and I saw that we were both trying to solve a similar technical problem," Kenny says. "Then I worked through mutual friends to meet their CEO and arranged for the right people on his team to meet with their Akamai counterparts."

Presidents and CEOs aren't the only executives building bridges between their organizations and the outside world nowadays. Take Beth Comstock, the chief marketing officer of General Electric. She is famous for her weekly "BlackBerry Beth" blog, in which she shares what she has learned in her external role for busy (and perhaps more internally focused) GE managers. The pithy and provocative blog goes out to thousands of GE's sales, marketing, and technology leaders. In it, Comstock passes along interesting information that people might have missed, taking care to tie it back to challenges and opportunities GE faces. For example, in a recent post from the World Economic Forum, she reported that a panel of scientists had come to the same conclusion that a GE survey had—that technology alone cannot ensure innovation and that more training in creativity is needed.

"I work hard to curate information that I don't believe many at GE will have heard and to translate information in a way that is relevant to our challenges," says Comstock. "I probably spend half of my time immersed in worlds beyond GE. I hope this encourages my colleagues to be more externally focused. The message is 'If I find it important to spend some of my time this way, maybe you will, too.'"

To connect their organizations to the wider world, collaborative leaders develop contacts not only in the typical areas—local clubs, industry associations, and customer and supplier relations—but beyond them. Networking in adjacent industries, innovation hot spots like Silicon Valley, or emerging economies or with people of different educational or ethnic backgrounds helps open their eyes to new business opportunities and partners. For example, Comstock's external contacts in the innovation space led GE to NASA, with which the corporation has shared insights and best practices. The two organizations have also begun discussions about space technologies that might have applications in health care.

6.   Engage Talent at the Periphery

Research has consistently shown that diverse teams produce better results, provided they are well led. The ability to bring together people from different backgrounds, disciplines, cultures, and generations and leverage all they have to offer, therefore, is a must-have for leaders. Yet many companies spend inordinate amounts of time, money, and energy attracting talented employees only to subject them to homogenizing processes that kill creativity. In a lot of multinational companies, for example, nonnative English speakers are at a disadvantage. To senior management, they don't sound as "leader-like" as the Anglophones, and they end up getting passed over for promotions. At a time when innovations are increasingly originating in emerging markets, companies that allow this to happen lose out.

France's Danone, one of the top performers in our research, makes sure its executives don't encounter such obstacles. When all the managers worldwide get together for the company's annual strategic review, many choose to present in their native tongue. Says CEO Franck Riboud: "We spend a fortune on interpreters so that being less articulate in English is not a barrier. Some of our executives have even presented their business case in native dress. This helps us steal away talent from competitors where those who don't speak perfect English get stuck."

Reckitt Benckiser, the UK-based producer of home, health, and personal care products and another top performer in our research, considers the diversity of its workforce to be one of its competitive advantages—and a key reason it has seen net income grow 17% annually, on average, from 1999 to 2010. No nationality dominates the company's senior team. Two executives are Dutch, one is German, two are British, one is South African, two are Italian, and one is from India. According to (soon-to-retire) CEO Bart Becht: "It doesn't matter whether I have a Pakistani, a Chinese person, a Brit, or a Turk, man or woman, sitting in the same room, or whether I have people from sales or something else, so long as I have people with different experiences because the chance for new ideas is much greater when you have people with different backgrounds. The chance for conflict is also higher—and conflict is good per se, as long as it's constructive and gets us to the best idea."

As Becht suggests, nationality isn't the only kind of diversity that matters. Research on creative industries shows that the collaborations that are most successful (whether in terms of patent citation, critical acclaim, or financial return) include both experienced people and newcomers and bring together people who haven't worked with one another before. Leaders need to make a concerted effort to promote this mix: Left to their own devices, people will choose to collaborate with others they know well or who have similar backgrounds. Static groups breed insularity, which can be deadly for innovation. Nokia's former executive team, for example, was 100% Finnish and had worked closely together for more than a decade. Many believe homogeneity explains why the team failed to see the smartphone threat emerging from Silicon Valley.

Left to their own devices, people will choose to collaborate with others they know well which can be deadly for innovation.

Collaborative leaders ensure that teams stay fresh via periodic infusions of new players. Including employees from Generation Y—those born from the mid-1970s to the early 2000s, who have grown up sharing knowledge and opinions online—is another obvious way to enliven collaborations. A number of leading companies have begun using technology to harness Gen Y ideas and perspectives. Salesforce.com, as we have seen, brought them in from the periphery by using Chatter to open its management off-site to all staff. At India's HCL, employees throughout the company join virtual conversations on topics that are important to them, and CEO Vineet Nayar reaches out personally through a popular blog that allows him to interact with a broad cross section of employees. In a market where the competition for engineering talent is fierce, the ability to attract the best and brightest helped HCL grow 30% annually from 2008 to 2010.

7.   Collaborate at the Top First

It's not enough for leaders to spot collaborative opportunities and attract the best talent to them. They must also set the tone by being good collaborators themselves. All too often, efforts to collaborate in the middle are sabotaged by political games and turf battles higher up in the organization. Consider that Microsoft, according to a former company executive writing in the *New York Times* last year, developed a viable tablet computer more than a decade ago but failed to preempt Apple's smash hit because competing Microsoft divisions conspired to kill the project.

Part of the problem is that many leadership teams, composed of the CEO and his or her direct reports, actually don't operate as teams. Each member runs his or her own region, function, or product or service category, without much responsibility—or incentive—for aligning the organization's various projects and operations into a coherent whole.

Collaboration Does Not Equal Consensus

Collaborative leadership is the capacity to engage people and groups outside one's formal control and inspire them to work toward common goals despite differences in convictions, cultural values, and operating norms.

Most people understand intuitively that collaborative leadership is the opposite of the old command-and-control model, but the differences with a consensus-based approach are more nuanced. Below are some helpful distinctions between the three leadership styles.

At Brazil's Natura Cosméticos, CEO Alessandro Carlucci has instituted a comprehensive "engagement process" that promotes a collaborative mind-set at all levels and has helped the firm win a top spot on *Fortune*'s list of best companies for leaders. The process was implemented after Natura's highly successful IPO in 2004, when competing agendas among the senior managers began to threaten the company's prospects. Carlucci decided he needed to reorganize the executive committee to unify its members around common goals and stop the power struggles. He asked the members of the top team to make a commitment to self-development as part of their stewardship of the company.

Each executive embarked on a "personal journey" with an external coach, who met with everyone individually and with the team as a group. "It is a different type of coaching," Carlucci explains. "It's not just talking to your boss or subordinates but talking about a person's life history, with their families; it is more holistic, broader, integrating all the different roles of a human being."

Roberto Pedote, Natura's senior vice president for finance, IT, and legal affairs, adds: "I think that the main point is that we are making ourselves vulnerable, showing that we are not supermen, that we have failures; that we are afraid of some things and we don't have all the answers."

COMPARING THREE STYLES OF LEADERSHIP

	COMMAND AND CONTROL	CONSENSUS	COLLABORATIVE
ORGANIZATIONAL STRUCTURE	Hierarchy	Matrix or small group	Dispersed, cross-organizational network
WHO HAS THE RELEVANT INFORMATION?	Senior management	Formally designated members or representatives of the relevant geographies and disciplines	Employees at all levels and locations and a variety of external stakeholders
WHO HAS THE AUTHORITY TO MAKE FINAL DECISIONS?	The people at the top of the organization have clear authority	All parties have equal authority	The people leading collaborations have clear authority
WHAT IS THE BASIS FOR ACCOUNTABILITY AND CONTROL?	Financial results against plan	Many performance indicators, by function or geography	Performance on achieving shared goals
WHERE DOES IT WORK BEST?	Works well within a defined hierarchy; works poorly for complex organizations and when innovation is important	Works in small teams; works poorly when speed is important	Works well for diverse groups and cross-unit and cross-company work, and when innovation and creativity are critical

Since the engagement process was adopted, Natura's executives have become much better at teaming up on efforts to improve the business, which grew by 21% in 2010. The collaborative mind-set at the top has cascaded down to the rest of the organization, and the process has been rolled out to all the company's managers.

If leaders are to encourage more innovation through partnerships across sectors and with suppliers, customers, and consumers, they need to stop relying heavily on short-term performance indicators. According to the psychologist Carol Dweck, people are driven to do tasks by either performance or learning goals. When performance goals dominate an environment, people are motivated to show others that they have a valued attribute, such as intelligence or leadership. When learning goals dominate, they are motivated to *develop* the attribute. Performance goals, she finds, induce people to favor tasks that will make them look good over tasks that will help them learn. A shift toward learning goals will make managers more open to exploring opportunities to acquire knowledge from others.

At HCL, CEO Vineet Nayar demonstrated his commitment to collaboration by adopting a radically different 360-degree evaluation for his top managers—one that invited a wide range of employees to weigh in. Although the company had done 360-degree reviews before, each manager had been assessed by a relatively small number of people, mostly within the manager's immediate span of control. As Nayar recalls in his book *Employees First, Customers Second* (Harvard Business Review Press, 2010), "most of the respondents operated within the same area as the person they were evaluating. This reinforced the boundaries between the parts of the pyramid. But we were trying to change all that. We wanted to encourage people to operate across these boundaries." Nayar set the tone by posting his own 360 degree evaluation on the web. Once executives got used to the new transparency, the 360-degree reviews were expanded to a broader group. A new feature, "Happy Feet," was added, allowing all employees whom a manager might affect or influence to evaluate that manager regardless of their reporting relationship.

Depoliticizing senior management so that executives are rewarded for collaborating rather than promoting their individual agendas is an absolute essential. At Reckitt Benckiser, there's little tolerance for politics. Says Bart Becht: "We go out of our way to make sure that politics get eradicated, because I think they're very bad for an organization. I think they're poison, to be honest with you." Becht's direct, no-nonsense style and the expectation that people should openly disagree with one another in meetings also help keep politics to a minimum, allowing real teamwork to take hold.

8.   Show a Strong Hand

Once leaders start getting employees to collaborate, they face a different problem: overdoing it. Too often people will try to collaborate on everything and wind up in endless meetings, debating ideas and struggling to find consensus. They can't reach decisions and execute quickly. Collaboration becomes not the oil greasing the wheel but the sand grinding it to a halt.

When people try to collaborate on everything, they can wind up in endless meetings, debating ideas and struggling to find consensus.

Effective collaborative leaders assume a strong role directing teams. They maintain agility by forming and disbanding them as opportunities come and go—in much the same way that Hollywood producers, directors, actors, writers, and technicians establish teams for the life of movie projects. Collaborative efforts are highly fluid and not confined to company silos.

Effective leaders also assign clear decision rights and responsibilities, so that at the appropriate point someone can end the discussion and make a final call. Although constructive confrontation and tempered disagreements are encouraged, battles aren't left raging on. This is exactly how things work at Reckitt Benckiser. When teams meet, people know that it is OK—in fact expected—to propose ideas and challenge one another. They debate loudly and furiously until the best idea wins. If no obvious agreement is reached in time, the person chairing the meeting normally makes a decision and the rest of the group falls in line. This ensures vigorous debate but clear decisions and quick action—diversity in counsel, unity in command, as Cyrus the Great once said.

9.   Loosening Control Without Losing Control

In the old world of silos and solo players, leaders had access to everything they needed under one roof, and a command-and-control style served them well. But things have changed: The world has become much more interconnected, and if executives don't know how to tap into the power of those connections, they'll be left behind.

Leaders today must be able to harness ideas, people, and resources from across boundaries of all kinds. That requires reinventing their talent strategies and building strong connections both inside and outside their organizations. To get all the disparate players to work together effectively, they also need to know when to wield influence rather than authority to move things forward, and when to halt unproductive discussions, squash politicking, and make final calls.

Differences in convictions, cultural values, and operating norms inevitably add complexity to collaborative efforts. But they also make them richer, more innovative, and more valuable. Getting that value is the heart of collaborative leadership.

CHAPTER 2

Want Collaboration?: Accept and Actively Manage Conflict

Companies try all kinds of ways to improve collaboration among different parts of the organization: cross-unit incentive systems, organizational restructuring, teamwork training. While these initiatives produce occasional success stories, most have only limited impact in dismantling organizational silos and fostering collaboration.

The problem? Most companies focus on the symptoms ("Sales and delivery do not work together as closely as they should") rather than on the root cause of failures in cooperation: conflict. The fact is, you can't improve collaboration until you've addressed the issue of conflict. The authors offer six strategies for effectively managing conflict:

- Devise and implement a common method for resolving conflict.
- Provide people with criteria for making trade-offs.
- Use the escalation of conflict as an opportunity for coaching.
- Establish and enforce a requirement of joint escalation.
- Ensure that managers resolve escalated conflicts directly with their counterparts.
- Make the process for escalated conflict-resolution transparent.

The first three strategies focus on the point of conflict; the second three focus on escalation of conflict up the management chain. Together they constitute a framework for effectively managing discord, one that integrates conflict resolution into day-to-day decision-making processes, thereby removing a barrier to cross-organizational collaboration.

The challenge is a long-standing one for senior managers: How do you get people in your organization to work together across internal boundaries? But the question has taken on urgency in today's global and fast-changing business environment. To service multinational accounts, you increasingly need seamless collaboration across geographic boundaries. To improve customer satisfaction, you increasingly need collaboration among functions ranging from R&D to distribution. To offer solutions tailored to customers' needs, you increasingly need collaboration between product and service groups.

Meanwhile, as competitive pressures continually force companies to find ways to do more with less, few managers have the luxury of relying on their own dedicated staffs to accomplish their objectives. Instead, most must work with and through people across the organization, many of whom have different priorities, incentives, and ways of doing things.

Getting collaboration right promises tremendous benefits: a unified face to customers, faster internal decision making, reduced costs through shared resources, and the development of more innovative products. But despite the billions of dollars spent on initiatives to improve collaboration, few companies are happy with the results. Time and again we have seen management teams employ the same few strategies to boost internal cooperation. They restructure their organizations and reengineer their business processes. They create cross-unit incentives. They offer teamwork training. While such initiatives yield the occasional success story, most of them have only limited impact in dismantling organizational silos and fostering collaboration and many are total failures.

The Three Myths of Collaboration

Companies attempt to foster collaboration among different parts of their organizations through a variety of methods, many based on a number of seemingly sensible but ultimately misguided assumptions:

A.   **Effective collaboration means "teaming."**

Many companies think that teamwork training is the way to promote collaboration across an organization. So they'll get the HR department to run hundreds of managers and their subordinates through intensive two- or three-day training programs. Workshops will offer techniques for getting groups aligned around common goals, for clarifying roles and responsibilities, for operating according to a shared set of behavioral norms, and so on.

Unfortunately, such workshops are usually the right solution to the wrong problems. First, the most critical breakdowns in collaboration typically occur not on actual teams but in the rapid and unstructured interactions between different groups within the organization. For example, someone from R&D will spend weeks unsuccessfully trying to get help from manufacturing to run a few tests on a new prototype. Meanwhile, people in manufacturing begin to complain about arrogant engineers from R&D expecting them to drop everything to help with another one of R&D's pet projects. Clearly, the need for collaboration extends to areas other than a formal team.

The second problem is that breakdowns in collaboration almost always result from fundamental differences among business functions and divisions. Teamwork training offers little guidance on how to work together in the context of competing objectives and limited resources. Indeed, the frequent emphasis on common goals further stigmatizes the idea of conflict in organizations where an emphasis on "polite" behavior regularly prevents effective problem solving. People who need to collaborate more effectively usually don't need to align around and work toward a common goal. They need to quickly and creatively solve problems by managing the inevitable conflict so that it works in their favor.

B.   **An effective incentive system will ensure collaboration.**

It's a tantalizing proposition: You can hardwire collaboration into your organization by rewarding collaborative behavior. Salespeople receive bonuses not only for hitting targets for their own division's products but also for hitting cross-selling targets. Staff in corporate support functions like IT and procurement have part of their bonuses determined by positive feedback from their internal clients.

Unfortunately, the results of such programs are usually disappointing. Despite greater financial incentives, for example, salespeople continue to focus on the sales of their own products to the detriment of selling integrated solutions. Employees continue to perceive the IT and procurement departments as difficult to work with, too focused on their own priorities. Why such poor results? To some extent, it's because individuals think—for the most part correctly—that if they perform well in their own operation they will be "taken care of" by their bosses. In addition, many people find that the costs of working with individuals in other parts of the organization—the extra time required, the aggravation—greatly outweigh the rewards for doing so.

Certainly, misaligned incentives can be a tremendous obstacle to cross-boundary collaboration. But even the most carefully constructed incentives won't eliminate tensions between people with competing business objectives. An incentive is too blunt an instrument to enable optimal resolution of the hundreds of different trade-offs that need to be made in a complex organization. What's more, overemphasis on incentives can create a culture in which people say, "If the company wanted me to do that, they would build it into my comp plan." Ironically, focusing on incentives as a means to encourage collaboration can end up undermining it.

C. **Organizations can be structured for collaboration.**

Many managers look for structural and procedural solutions—cross-functional task forces, collaborative "groupware," complex webs of dotted reporting lines on the organization chart—to create greater internal collaboration. But bringing people together is very different from getting them to collaborate.

Consider the following scenario. Individual information technology departments have been stripped out of a company's business units and moved to a corporatewide, shared-services IT organization. Senior managers rightly recognize that this kind of change is a recipe for conflict because various groups will now essentially compete with one another for scarce IT resources. So managers try mightily to design conflict out of, and collaboration into, the new organization. For example, to enable collaborative decision making within IT and between IT and the business units, business units are required to enter requests for IT support into a computerized tracking system. The system is designed to enable managers within the IT organization to prioritize projects and optimally deploy resources to meet the various requests.

Despite painstaking process design, results are disappointing. To avoid the inevitable conflicts between business units and IT over project prioritization, managers in the business units quickly learn to bring their requests to those they know in the IT organization rather than entering the requests into the new system. Consequently, IT professionals assume that any project in the system is a lower priority further discouraging use of the system. People's inability to deal effectively with conflict has undermined a new process specifically designed to foster organizational collaboration.

So what's the problem? Most companies respond to the challenge of improving collaboration in entirely the wrong way. They focus on the symptoms ("Sales and delivery do not work together as closely as they should") rather than on the root cause of failures in cooperation: conflict. The fact is, you can't improve collaboration until you've addressed the issue of conflict.

This can come as a surprise to even the most experienced executives, who generally don't fully appreciate the inevitability of conflict in complex organizations. And even if they do recognize this, many mistakenly assume that efforts to increase collaboration will significantly reduce that conflict, when in fact some of these efforts—for example, restructuring initiatives—actually produce more of it.

Executives underestimate not only the inevitability of conflict but also and this is key—its importance to the organization. The disagreements sparked by differences in perspective, competencies, access to information, and strategic focus within a company actually generate much of the value that can come from collaboration across organizational boundaries. Clashes between parties are the crucibles in which creative solutions are developed and wise trade-offs among competing objectives are made. So instead of trying simply to reduce disagreements, senior executives need to embrace conflict and, just as important, institutionalize mechanisms for managing it.

Clashes between parties are the crucibles in which creative solutions are developed and wise trade-offs among competing objectives are made.

Even though most people lack an innate understanding of how to deal with conflict effectively, there are a number of straightforward ways that executives can help their people—and their organizations—constructively manage it. These can be divided into two main areas: strategies for managing disagreements at the point of conflict and strategies for managing conflict upon escalation up the management chain. These methods can help a company move through the conflict that is a necessary precursor to truly effective collaboration and, more important, extract the value that often lies latent in intraorganizational differences. When companies are able to do both, conflict is transformed from a major liability into a significant asset.

Strategies for Managing Disagreements at the Point of Conflict

Conflict management works best when the parties involved in a disagreement are equipped to manage it themselves. The aim is to get people to resolve issues on their own through a process that improves—or at least does not damage—their relationships. The following strategies help produce decisions that are better informed and more likely to be implemented.

Devise and implement a common method for resolving conflict.

Consider for a moment the hypothetical Matrix Corporation, a composite of many organizations we've worked with whose challenges will likely be familiar to managers. Over the past few years, salespeople from nearly a dozen of Matrix's product and service groups have been called on to design and sell integrated solutions to their customers. For any given sale, five or more lead salespeople and their teams have to agree on issues of resource allocation, solution design, pricing, and sales strategy. Not surprisingly, the teams are finding this difficult. Who should contribute the most resources to a particular customer's offering? Who should reduce the scope of their participation or discount their pricing to meet a customer's budget? Who should defer when disagreements arise about account strategy? Who should manage key relationships within the customer account? Indeed, given these thorny questions, Matrix is finding that a single large sale typically generates far more conflict inside the company than it does with the customer. The resulting wasted time and damaged relationships among sales teams are making it increasingly difficult to close sales.

Most companies face similar sorts of problems. And, like Matrix, they leave employees to find their own ways of resolving them. But without a structured method for dealing with these issues, people get bogged down not only in what the right result should be but also in how to arrive at it. Often, they will avoid or work around conflict, thereby forgoing important opportunities to collaborate. And when people do decide to confront their differences, they usually default to the approach they know best: debating about who's right and who's wrong or haggling over small concessions. Among the negative consequences of such approaches are suboptimal, "split-the-difference" resolutions if not outright deadlock.

Establishing a companywide process for resolving disagreements can alter this familiar scenario. At the very least, a well-defined, well-designed conflict resolution method will reduce transaction costs, such as wasted time and the accumulation of ill will, that often come with the struggle to work though differences. At best, it will yield the innovative outcomes that are likely to emerge from discussions that draw on a multitude of objectives and perspectives. There is an array of conflict resolution methods a company can use. But to be effective, they should offer a clear, step-by-step process for parties to follow. They should also be made an integral part of existing business activities—account planning, sourcing, R&D budgeting, and the like. If conflict resolution is set up as a separate, exception-based process—a kind of organizational appeals court—it will likely wither away once initial managerial enthusiasm wanes.

At Intel, new employees learn a common method and language for decision making and conflict resolution. The company puts them through training in which they learn to use a variety of tools for handling discord. Not only does the training show that top management sees disagreements as an inevitable aspect of doing business, it also provides a common framework that expedites conflict resolution. Little time is wasted in figuring out the best way to handle a disagreement or trading accusations about "not being a team player"; guided by this clearly defined process, people can devote their time and energy to exploring and constructively evaluating a variety of options for how to move forward. Intel's systematic method for working through differences has helped sustain some of the company's hallmark

11

qualities: innovation, operational efficiency, and the ability to make and implement hard decisions in the face of complex strategic choices.

Provide people with criteria for making trade-offs.

At our hypothetical Matrix Corporation, senior managers overseeing cross-unit sales teams often admonish those teams to "do what's right for the customer." Unfortunately, this exhortation isn't much help when conflict arises. Given Matrix's ability to offer numerous combinations of products and services, company managers—each with different training and experience and access to different information, not to mention different unit priorities—have, not surprisingly, different opinions about how best to meet customers' needs. Similar clashes in perspective result when exasperated senior managers tell squabbling team members to set aside their differences and "put Matrix's interests first." That's because it isn't always clear what's best for the company given the complex interplay among Matrix's objectives for revenue, profitability, market share, and long-term growth.

Even when companies equip people with a common method for resolving conflict, employees often will still need to make zero-sum trade-offs between competing priorities. That task is made much easier and less contentious when top management can clearly articulate the criteria for making such choices. Obviously, it's not easy to reduce a company's strategy to clearly defined trade-offs, but it's worth trying. For example, salespeople who know that five points of market share are more important than a ten point increase on a customer satisfaction scale are much better equipped to make strategic concessions when the needs and priorities of different parts of the business conflict. And even when the criteria do not lead to a straightforward answer, the guidelines can at least foster productive conversations by providing an objective focus. Establishing such criteria also sends a clear signal from management that it views conflict as an inevitable result of managing a complex business.

At Blue Cross and Blue Shield of Florida, the strategic decision to rely more and more on alliances with other organizations has significantly increased the potential for disagreement in an organization long accustomed to developing capabilities in-house. Decisions about whether to build new capabilities, buy them outright, or gain access to them through alliances are natural flashpoints for conflict among internal groups. The health insurer might have tried to minimize such conflict through a structural solution, giving a particular group the authority to make decisions concerning whether, for instance, to develop a new claims-processing system in-house, to do so jointly with an alliance partner, or to license or acquire an existing system from a third party. Instead, the company established a set of criteria designed to help various groups within the organization—for example, the enterprise alliance group, IT, and marketing—to collectively make such decisions.

The criteria are embodied in a spreadsheet-type tool that guides people in assessing the trade-offs involved—say, between speed in getting a new process up and running versus ensuring its seamless integration with existing ones—when deciding whether to build, buy, or ally. People no longer debate back and forth across a table, advocating their preferred outcomes. Instead, they sit around the table and together apply a common set of trade-off criteria to the decision at hand. The resulting insights into the pros and cons of each approach enable more effective execution, no matter which path is chosen. (For a simplified version of the trade-off tool, see the exhibit "Blue Cross and Blue Shield: Build, Buy, or Ally?")

Blue Cross and Blue Shield: Build, Buy, or Ally?

One of the most effective ways senior managers can help resolve cross-unit conflict is by giving people the criteria for making trade-offs when the needs of different parts of the business are at odds with one another. At Blue Cross and Blue Shield of Florida, there are often conflicting perspectives over whether to build new capabilities (for example, a new claims-processing system, as in the hypothetical example below), acquire them, or gain access to them through an alliance. The company uses a grid-like poster (a simplified version of which is shown here) that helps multiple parties analyze the trade-offs associated with these three options. By checking various boxes in the grid using personalized markers, participants indicate how they assess a particular option against a variety of criteria: for example, the date by which the new capability needs to be implemented; the availability of internal resources such as capital and staff needed to develop the capability; and the degree of integration required with existing products and processes. The table format makes criteria and trade-offs easy to compare. The visual depiction of people's "votes" and the ensuing discussion help individuals see how their differences often arise from such factors as access to different data or different prioritizing of objectives. As debate unfolds—and as people move their markers in response to new information—they can see where they are aligned and where and why they separate into significant factions of disagreement. Eventually, the criteria-based dialogue tends to produce a preponderance of markers in one of the three rows, thus yielding operational consensus around a decision.

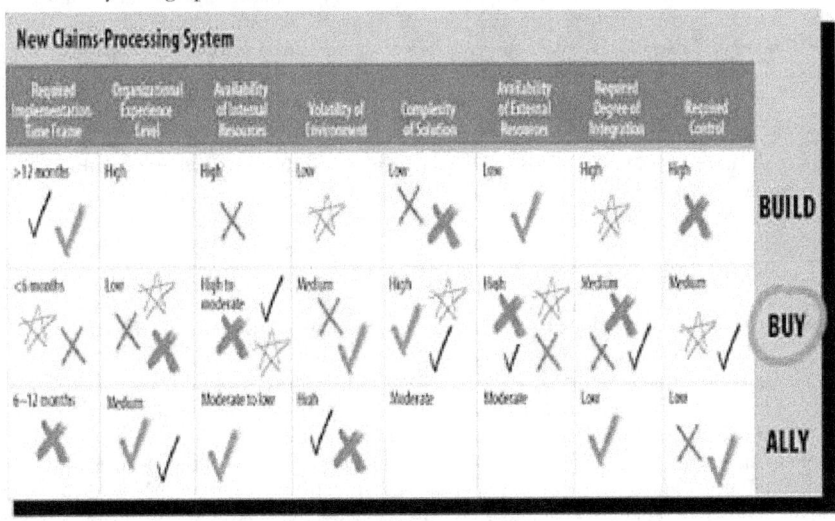

Use the escalation of conflict as an opportunity for coaching.

Managers at Matrix spend much of their time playing the organizational equivalent of hot potato. Even people who are new to the company learn within weeks that the best thing to do with cross-unit conflict is to toss it up the management chain. Immediate supervisors take a quick pass at resolving the dispute but, being busy themselves, usually pass it up to *their* supervisors. Those supervisors do the same, and before long the problem lands in the lap of a senior-level manager, who then spends much of his time resolving disagreements. Clearly, this isn't ideal. Because the senior managers are a number of steps removed from the source of the controversy, they rarely have a good understanding of the situation. Furthermore, the more time they spend resolving internal clashes, the less time they spend engaged in the business, and the more isolated they are from the very information they need to resolve the disputes dumped in their laps. Meanwhile, Matrix employees get so little opportunity to learn about how to deal with conflict that it becomes not only expedient but almost necessary for them to quickly bump conflict up the management chain.

While Matrix's story may sound extreme, we can hardly count the number of companies we've seen that operate this way. And even in the best of situations—for example, where a companywide conflict-management process is in place and where trade-off criteria are well understood—there is still a natural tendency for people to let their bosses sort out disputes. Senior managers contribute to this tendency by quickly resolving the problems presented to them. While this may be the fastest and easiest way to fix the problems, it encourages people to punt issues upstairs at the first sign of difficulty. Instead, managers should treat escalations as opportunities to help employees become better at resolving conflict. (For an example of how managers can help their employees improve their conflict resolution skills, see the exhibit "IBM: Coaching for Conflict.")

At KLA-Tencor, a major manufacturer of semiconductor production equipment, a materials executive in each division oversees a number of buyers who procure the materials and component parts for machines that the division makes. When negotiating a companywide contract with a supplier, a buyer often must work with the company commodity manager, as well as with buyers from other divisions who deal with the same supplier. There is often conflict, for example, over the delivery terms for components supplied to two or more divisions under the contract. In such cases, the commodity manager and the division materials executive will push the division buyer to consider the needs of the other divisions, alternatives that might best address the collective needs of the different divisions, and the standards to be applied in assessing the trade-offs between alternatives. The aim is to help the buyer see solutions that haven't yet been considered and to resolve the conflict with the buyer in the other division.

Initially, this approach required more time from managers than if they had simply made the decisions themselves. But it has paid off in fewer disputes that senior managers need to resolve, speedier contract negotiation, and improved contract terms both for the company as a whole and for multiple divisions. For example, the buyers from three KLA-Tencor product divisions recently locked horns over a global contract with a key supplier. At issue was the trade-off between two variables: one, the supplier's level of liability for materials it needs to purchase in order to fulfill orders and, two, the flexibility granted the KLA-Tencor divisions in modifying the size of the orders and their required lead times. Each division demanded a different balance between these two factors, and the buyers took the conflict to their managers, wondering if they should try to negotiate each of the different trade-offs into the contract or pick among them. After being coached to consider how each division's business model shaped its preference—and using this understanding to jointly brainstorm alternatives—the buyers and commodity manager arrived at a creative solution that worked for everyone: They would request a clause in the contract that allowed them to increase and decrease flexibility in order volume and lead time, with corresponding changes in supplier liability, as required by changing market conditions.

IBM: Coaching for Conflict

Managers can reduce the repeated escalation of conflict up the management chain by helping employees learn how to resolve disputes themselves. At IBM, executives get training in conflict management and are offered online resources to help them coach others. One tool on the corporate intranet (an edited excerpt of which is shown here) walks managers through a variety of conversations they might have with a direct report who is struggling to resolve a dispute with people from one or more groups in the company—some of whom, by design, will be consulted to get their views but won't be involved in negotiating the final decision.

Strategies for Managing Conflict upon Escalation

Equipped with common conflict resolution methods and trade-off criteria, and supported by systematic coaching, people are better able to resolve conflict on their own. But certain complex disputes will inevitably need to be decided by superiors. Consequently, managers must ensure that, upon escalation, conflict is resolved constructively and efficiently—and in ways that model desired behaviors.

If you hear from someone reporting to you that ...	The problem could be that ...	And you could help your report by saying something like...
"Everyone still insists on being a decision maker."	The people your report is dealing with remain concerned that unless they have a formal voice in making the decision—or a key piece of the decision—their needs and interests won't be taken into account.	"You might want to explain why people are being consulted and how this information will be used." "Are there ways to break this decision apart into a series of subissues and assign decision-making roles around those subissues?" "Consider talking to the group about the costs of having everyone involved in the final decision."
"If I consult with this person up front, he might try to force an answer on me or create roadblocks to my efforts to move forward."	The person you are coaching may be overlooking the risks of not asking for input—mainly, that any decision arrived at without input could be sabotaged later on.	"How would you ask someone for input? What would you tell her about your purpose in seeking it? What questions would you ask? What would you say if she put forth a solution and resisted discussing other options?" "Is there a way to manage the risk that she will try to block your efforts other than by not consulting her at all? If you consult with her now, might that in fact lower the risk that she will try to derail your efforts later?"
"I have consulted with all the right parties and have crafted, by all accounts, a good plan. But the decision makers cannot settle on a final decision."	The right people were included in the negotiating group, but the process for negotiating a final decision was not determined.	"What are the ground rules for how decisions will be made? Do all those in the group need to agree? Must the majority agree? Or just those with the greatest competence?" "What interests underlie the objective of having everyone agree? Is there another decision-making process that would meet those interests?"

Establish and enforce a requirement of joint escalation.

Let's again consider the situation at Matrix. In a typical conflict, three salespeople from different divisions become involved in a dispute over pricing. Frustrated, one of them decides to hand the problem up to his boss, explaining the situation in a short voice-mail message. The message offers little more than bare acknowledgment of the other salespeoples' viewpoints. The manager then determines, on the basis of what he knows about the situation, the solution to the problem. The salesperson, armed with his boss's decision, returns to his counterparts and shares with them the verdict—which, given the process, is simply a stronger version of the solution the salesperson had put forward in the first place. But wait! The other two salespeople have also gone to *their* managers and carried back stronger versions of *their* solutions. At this point, each salesperson is locked into what is now "my manager's view" of the right pricing scheme. The problem, already thorny, has become even more intractable.

The best way to avoid this kind of debilitating deadlock is for people to present a disagreement jointly to their boss or bosses. This will reduce or even eliminate the suspicion, surprises, and damaged personal relationships ordinarily associated with unilateral escalation. It will also guarantee that the ultimate decision maker has access to a wide array of perspectives on the conflict, its causes, and the various ways it might be resolved. Furthermore, companies that require people to share responsibility for the escalation of a conflict often see a decrease in the number of problems that are pushed up the management chain. Joint escalation helps create the kind of accountability that is lacking when people

15

know they can provide their side of an issue to their own manager and blame others when things don't work out.

A few years ago, after a merger that resulted in a much larger and more complex organization, senior managers at the Canadian telecommunications company Telus found themselves virtually paralyzed by a daily barrage of unilateral escalations. Just determining who was dealing with what and who should be talking to whom took up huge amounts of senior management's time. So the company made joint escalation a central tenet of its new organizationwide protocols for conflict resolution—a requirement given teeth by managers' refusal to respond to unilateral escalation. When a conflict occurred among managers in different departments concerning, say, the allocation of resources among the departments, the managers were required to jointly describe the problem, what had been done so far to resolve it, and its possible solutions. Then they had to send a joint write-up of the situation to each of their bosses and stand ready to appear together and answer questions when those bosses met to work through a solution. In many cases, the requirement of systematically documenting the conflict and efforts to resolve it—because it forced people to make such efforts—led to a problem being resolved on the spot, without having to be kicked upstairs. Within weeks, this process resulted in the resolution of hundreds of issues that had been stalled for months in the newly merged organization.

Ensure that managers resolve escalated conflicts directly with their counterparts.

Let's return to the three salespeople at Matrix who took their dispute over pricing to their respective bosses and then met again, only to find themselves further from agreement than before. So what did they do at that point? They sent the problem *back* to their bosses. These three bosses, each of whom thought he'd already resolved the issue, decided the easiest thing to do would be to escalate it themselves. This would save them time and put the conflict before senior managers with the broad view seemingly needed to make a decision. Unfortunately, by doing this, the three bosses simply perpetuated the situation their salespeople had created, putting forward a biased viewpoint and leaving it to their own managers to come up with an answer. In the end, the decision was made unilaterally by the senior manager with the most organizational clout. This result bred resentment back down the management chain. A sense of "we'll win next time" took hold, ensuring that future conflict would be even more difficult to resolve.

It's not unusual to see managers react to escalations from their employees by simply passing conflicts up their own functional or divisional chains until they reach a senior executive involved with all the affected functions or divisions. Besides providing a poor example for others in the organization, this can be disastrous for a company that needs to move quickly. To avoid wasting time, a manager somewhere along the chain might try to resolve the problem swiftly and decisively by herself. But this, too, has its costs. In a complex organization, where many issues have significant implications for numerous parts of the business, unilateral responses to unilateral escalations are a recipe for inefficiency, bad decisions, and ill feelings.

The solution to these problems is a commitment by managers—a commitment codified in a formal policy—to deal with escalated conflict directly with their counterparts. Of course, doing this can feel cumbersome, especially when an issue is time-sensitive. But resolving the problem early on is ultimately more efficient than trying to sort it out later, after a decision becomes known because it has negatively affected some part of the business.

In the 1990s, IBM's sales and delivery organization became increasingly complex as the company reintegrated previously independent divisions and reorganized itself to provide customers with full solutions of bundled products and services. Senior executives soon recognized that managers were not dealing with escalated conflicts and that relationships among them were strained because they failed to consult and coordinate around cross-unit issues. This led to the creation of a forum called the Market Growth Workshop (a name carefully chosen to send a message throughout the company that getting cross-unit conflict resolved was critical to meeting customer needs and, in turn, growing market share). These monthly conference calls brought together managers, salespeople, and frontline product specialists from across the company to discuss and resolve cross-unit conflicts that were hindering important sales—for example, the difficulty salespeople faced in getting needed technical resources from overstretched product groups.

The Market Growth Workshops weren't successful right away. In the beginning, busy senior managers, reluctant to spend time on issues that often hadn't been carefully thought through, began sending their subordinates to the meetings which made it even more difficult to resolve the problems discussed. So the company developed a simple preparation template that forced people to document and analyze disputes before the conference calls. Senior managers, realizing the problems created by their absence, recommitted themselves to attending the meetings. Over time, as complex conflicts were resolved during these sessions and significant sales were closed, attendees began to see these meetings as an opportunity to be involved in the resolution of high-stakes, high-visibility issues.

Make the process for escalated conflict resolution transparent.

When a sales conflict is resolved by a Matrix senior manager, the word comes down the management chain in the form of an action item: Put together an offering with this particular mix of products and services at these prices. The only elaboration may be an admonishment to "get the sales team together, work up a proposal, and get back to the customer as quickly as possible." The problem is solved, at least for the time being. But the salespeople unless they have been able to divine themes from the patterns of decisions made over time—are left with little guidance on how to resolve similar issues in the future. They may justifiably wonder: How was the decision made? Based on what kinds of assumptions? With what kinds of trade-offs? How might the reasoning change if the situation were different?

In most companies, once managers have resolved a conflict, they announce the decision and move on. The resolution process and rationale behind the decision are left inside a managerial black box. While it's rarely helpful for managers to share all the gory details of their deliberations around contentious issues, failing to take the time to explain how a decision was reached and the factors that went into it squanders a major opportunity. A frank discussion of the trade-offs involved in decisions would provide guidance to people trying to resolve conflicts in the future and would help nip in the bud the kind of speculation—who won and who lost, which managers or units have the most power—that breeds mistrust, sparks turf battles, and otherwise impedes cross-organizational collaboration. In general, clear communication about the resolution of the conflict can increase people's willingness and ability to implement decisions.

During the past two years, IBM's Market Growth Workshops have evolved into a more structured approach to managing escalated conflict, known as Cross-Team Workouts. Designed to make conflict resolution more transparent, the workouts are weekly meetings of people across the organization who work together on sales and delivery issues for specific accounts. The meetings provide a public forum for resolving conflicts over account strategy, solution configuration, pricing, and delivery. Those issues that cannot be resolved at the local level are escalated to regional workout sessions attended by managers from product groups, services, sales, and finance. Attendees then communicate and explain meeting resolutions to their reports. Issues that cannot be resolved at the regional level are escalated to an even higher-level workout meeting attended by cross-unit executives from a larger geographic region—like the Americas or Asia Pacific—and chaired by the general manager of the region presenting the issue. The most complex and strategic issues reach this global forum. The overlapping attendance at these sessions—in which the managers who chair one level of meeting attend sessions at the next level up, thereby observing the decision-making process at that stage—further enhances the transparency of the system among different levels of the company. IBM has further formalized the process for the direct resolution of conflicts between services and product sales on large accounts by designating a managing director in sales and a global relationship partner in IBM global services as the ultimate point of resolution for escalated conflicts. By explicitly making the resolution of complex conflicts part of the job descriptions for both managing director and global relationship partner—and by making that clear to others in the organization—IBM has reduced ambiguity, increased transparency, and increased the efficiency with which conflicts are resolved.

Tapping the Learning Latent in Conflict

The six strategies we have discussed constitute a framework for effectively managing organizational discord, one that integrates conflict resolution into day-to-day decision-making processes, thereby removing a critical barrier to cross-organizational collaboration. But the strategies also hint at something else: that conflict can be more than a necessary antecedent to collaboration.

Let's return briefly to Matrix. More than three-quarters of all cross-unit sales at the company trigger disputes about pricing. Roughly half of the sales lead to clashes over account control. A substantial number of sales also produce disagreements over the design of customer solutions, with the conflict often rooted in divisions' incompatible measurement systems and the concerns of some people about the quality of the solutions being assembled. But managers are so busy trying to resolve these almost daily disputes that they don't see the patterns or sources of conflict. Interestingly, if they ever wanted to identify patterns like these, Matrix managers might find few signs of them. That's because salespeople, who regularly hear their bosses complain about all the disagreements in the organization, have concluded that they'd better start shielding their superiors from discord.

The situation at Matrix is not unusual—most companies view conflict as an unnecessary nuisance—but that view is unfortunate. When a company begins to see conflict as a valuable resource that should be managed and exploited, it is likely to gain insight into problems that senior managers may not have known existed. Because internal friction is often caused by unaddressed strains within an organization or between an organization and its environment, setting up methods to track conflict and examine its causes can provide an interesting new perspective on a variety of issues. In the case of Matrix, taking the time to aggregate the experiences of individual salespeople involved in recurring disputes would likely lead to better approaches to setting prices, establishing incentives for salespeople, and monitoring the company's quality control process.

At Johnson & Johnson, an organization that has a highly decentralized structure, conflict is recognized as a positive aspect of cross-company collaboration. For example, a small internal group charged with facilitating sourcing collaboration among J&J's independent operating companies—particularly their outsourcing of clinical research services—actively works to extract lessons from conflicts. The group tracks and analyzes disagreements about issues such as what to outsource, whether and how to shift spending among suppliers, and what supplier capabilities to invest in. It hosts a council, comprising representatives from the various operating companies, that meets regularly to discuss these differences and explore their strategic implications. As a result, trends in clinical research outsourcing are spotted and information about them is disseminated throughout J&J more quickly. The operating companies benefit from insights about new offshoring opportunities, technologies, and ways of structuring collaboration with suppliers. And J&J, which can now piece together an accurate and global view of its suppliers, is better able to partner with them. Furthermore, the company realizes more value from its relationship with suppliers—yet another example of how the effective management of conflict can ultimately lead to fruitful collaboration.

J&J's approach is unusual but not unique. The benefits it offers provide further evidence that conflict—so often viewed as a liability to be avoided whenever possible—can be valuable to a company that knows how to manage it.

CHAPTER 3

Eight Ways to Build Collaborative Teams

Executing complex initiatives like acquisitions or an IT overhaul requires a breadth of knowledge that can be provided only by teams that are large, diverse, virtual, and composed of highly educated specialists. The irony is, those same characteristics have an alarming tendency to decrease collaboration on a team. What's a company to do?

Gratton, a London Business School professor, and Erickson, president of the Concours Institute, studied 55 large teams and identified those with strong collaboration despite their complexity. Examining the team dynamics and environment at firms ranging from Royal Bank of Scotland to Nokia to Marriott, the authors isolated eight success factors: (1) *"Signature" relationship practices* that build bonds among the staff, in memorable ways that are particularly suited to a company's business. (2) *Role models of collaboration* among executives, which help cooperation trickle down to the staff. (3) *The establishment of a "gift culture,"* in which managers support employees by mentoring them daily, instead of a transactional "tit-for-tat culture." (4) *Training in relationship skills,* such as communication and conflict resolution. (5) *A sense of community,* which corporate HR can foster by sponsoring group activities. (6) *Ambidextrous leadership,* or leaders who are both task-oriented and relationship-oriented. (7) *Good use of heritage relationships,* by populating teams with members who know and trust one another. (8) *Role clarity and task ambiguity,* achieved by defining individual roles sharply but giving teams latitude on approach.

As teams have grown from a standard of 20 members to comprise 100 or more, team practices that once worked well no longer apply. The new complexity of teams requires companies to increase their capacity for collaboration, by making long-term investments that build relationships and trust, and smart near-term decisions about how teams are formed and run.

When tackling a major initiative like an acquisition or an overhaul of IT systems, companies rely on large, diverse teams of highly educated specialists to get the job done. These teams often are convened quickly to meet an urgent need and work together virtually, collaborating online and sometimes over long distances.

Appointing such a team is frequently the only way to assemble the knowledge and breadth required to pull off many of the complex tasks businesses face today. When the BBC covers the World Cup or the Olympics, for instance, it gathers a large team of researchers, writers, producers, cameramen, and technicians, many of whom have not met before the project. These specialists work together under the high pressure of a "no retake" environment, with just one chance to record the action. Similarly, when the central IT team at Marriott sets out to develop sophisticated systems to enhance guest experiences, it has to collaborate closely with independent hotel owners, customer-experience experts, global brand managers, and regional heads, each with his or her own agenda and needs.

Our recent research into team behavior at 15 multinational companies, however, reveals an interesting paradox: Although teams that are large, virtual, diverse, and composed of highly educated specialists are increasingly crucial with challenging projects, those same four characteristics make it hard for teams to get anything done. To put it another way, the qualities required for success are the same qualities that undermine success. Members of complex teams are less likely—*absent other influences*—to share knowledge freely, to learn from one another, to shift workloads flexibly to break up unexpected bottlenecks, to help one another complete jobs and meet deadlines, and to share resources—in other words, to

20

collaborate. They are less likely to say that they "sink or swim" together, want one another to succeed, or view their goals as compatible.

The Research

Our work is based on a major research initiative conducted jointly by the Concours Institute (a member of BSG Alliance) and the Cooperative Research Project of London Business School, with funding from the Advanced Institute for Management and 15 corporate sponsors. The initiative was created as a way to explore the practicalities of collaborative work in contemporary organizations.

We sent surveys to 2,420 people, including members of 55 teams. A total of 1,543 people replied, a response rate of 64%. Separate surveys were administered to group members, to group leaders, to the executives who evaluated teams, and to HR leaders at the companies involved. The tasks performed by the teams included new-product development, process reengineering, and identifying new solutions to business problems. The companies involved included four telecommunication companies, seven financial services or consulting firms, two media companies, a hospitality firm, and one oil company. The size of the teams ranged from four to 183 people, with an average of 44.

Our objective was to study the levers that executives could pull to improve team performance and innovation in collaborative tasks. We examined scores of possible factors, including the following:

The general culture of the company. We designed a wide range of survey questions to measure the extent to which the firm had a cooperative culture and to uncover employees' attitudes toward knowledge sharing.

Human resources practices and processes. We studied the way staffing took place and the process by which people were promoted. We examined the extent and type of training, how reward systems were configured, and the extent to which mentoring and coaching took place.

Socialization and network-building practices. We looked at how often people within the team participated in informal socialization, and the type of interaction that was most common. We also asked numerous questions about the extent to which team members were active in informal communities.

The design of the task. We asked team members and team leaders about the task itself. Our interest here was in how they perceived the purpose of the task, how complex it was, the extent to which the task required members of the team to be interdependent, and the extent to which the task required them to engage in boundary-spanning activities with people outside the team.

The leadership of the team. We studied the perceptions team members had of their leaders' style and how the leaders described their own style. In particular, we were interested in the extent to which the leaders practiced relationship-oriented and task-oriented skills and set cooperative or competitive goals.

The behavior of the senior executives. We asked team members and team leaders about their perceptions of the senior executives of their business unit. We focused in particular on whether team members described them as cooperative or competitive.

In total we considered more than 100 factors. Using a range of statistical analyses, we were able to identify eight that correlated with the successful performance of teams handling complex collaborative tasks. (See the sidebar "Eight Factors That Lead to Success.")

Consider the issue of size. Teams have grown considerably over the past ten years. New technologies help companies extend participation on a project to an ever greater number of people, allowing firms to tap into a wide body of knowledge and expertise. A decade or so ago, the common view was that true teams rarely had more than 20 members. Today, according to our research, many complex tasks involve teams of 100 or more. However, as the size of a team increases beyond 20 members, the tendency to collaborate naturally decreases, we have found. Under the right conditions, large teams can achieve high levels of cooperation, but creating those conditions requires thoughtful, and sometimes significant, investments in the capacity for collaboration across the organization.

Working together virtually has a similar impact on teams. The majority of those we studied had members spread among multiple locations—in several cases, in as many as 13 sites around the globe. But as teams became more virtual, we saw, cooperation also declined, unless the company had taken measures to establish a collaborative culture.

As for diversity, the challenging tasks facing businesses today almost always require the input and expertise of people with disparate views and backgrounds to create cross-fertilization that sparks insight and innovation. But diversity also creates problems. Our research shows that team members collaborate more easily and naturally if they perceive themselves as being alike. The differences that inhibit collaboration include not only nationality but also age, educational level, and even tenure. Greater diversity also often means that team members are working with people that they know only superficially or have never met before—colleagues drawn from other divisions of the company, perhaps, or even from outside it. We have found that the higher the proportion of strangers on the team and the greater the diversity of background and experience, the less likely the team members are to share knowledge or exhibit other collaborative behaviors.

In the same way, the higher the educational level of the team members is, the more challenging collaboration appears to be for them. We found that the greater the proportion of experts a team had, the more likely it was to disintegrate into nonproductive conflict or stalemate.

We found that the greater the proportion of experts a team had, the more likely it was to disintegrate into nonproductive conflict or stalemate.

So how can executives strengthen an organization's ability to perform complex collaborative tasks—to maximize the effectiveness of large, diverse teams, while minimizing the disadvantages posed by their structure and composition?

Collaboration Conundrums

Four traits that are crucial to teams—but also undermine them

Large Size

Whereas a decade ago, teams rarely had more than 20 members, our findings show that their size has increased significantly, no doubt because of new technologies. Large teams are often formed to ensure the involvement of a wide stakeholder group, the coordination of a diverse set of activities, and the harnessing of multiple skills. As a consequence, many inevitably involve 100 people or more. However, our research shows that as the size of the team increases beyond 20 members, the level of natural cooperation among members of the team decreases.

Virtual Participation

Today most complex collaborative teams have members who are working at a distance from one another. Again, the logic is that the assigned tasks require the insights and knowledge of people from many locations. Team members may be working in offices in the same city or strung across the world. Only 40% of the teams in our sample had members all in one place. Our research shows that as teams become more virtual, collaboration declines.

Diversity

Often the challenging tasks facing today's businesses require the rapid assembly of people from multiple backgrounds and perspectives, many of whom have rarely, if ever, met. Their diverse knowledge and views can spark insight and innovation. However, our research shows that the higher the proportion of people who don't know anyone else on the team and the greater the diversity, the less likely the team members are to share knowledge.

High Education Levels

Complex collaborative teams often generate huge value by drawing on a variety of deeply specialized skills and knowledge to devise new solutions. Again, however, our research shows that the greater the proportion of highly educated specialists on a team, the more likely the team is to disintegrate into unproductive conflicts.

To answer that question we looked carefully at 55 large teams and identified those that demonstrated high levels of collaborative behavior despite their complexity. Put differently, they succeeded both because of and despite their composition. Using a range of statistical analyses, we considered how more than 100 factors, such as the design of the task and the company culture, might contribute to collaboration, manifested, for example, in a willingness to share knowledge and workloads. Out of the 100-plus factors, we were able to isolate eight practices that correlated with success—that is, that appeared to help teams overcome substantially the difficulties that were posed by size, long-distance communication, diversity, and specialization. We then interviewed the teams that were very strong in these practices, to find out how they did it. In this article we'll walk through the practices. They fall into four general categories—executive support, HR practices, the strength of the team leader, and the structure of the team itself.

Eight Factors That Lead to Success

1. Investing in signature relationship practices. Executives can encourage collaborative behavior by making highly visible investments—in facilities with open floor plans to foster communication, for example—that demonstrate their commitment to collaboration.

2. Modeling collaborative behavior. At companies where the senior executives demonstrate highly collaborative behavior themselves, teams collaborate well.

3. Creating a "gift culture." Mentoring and coaching—especially on an informal basis— help people build the networks they need to work across corporate boundaries.

4. Ensuring the requisite skills. Human resources departments that teach employees how to build relationships, communicate well, and resolve conflicts creatively can have a major impact on team collaboration.

5. Supporting a strong sense of community. When people feel a sense of community, they are more comfortable reaching out to others and more likely to share knowledge.

6. Assigning team leaders that are both task- and relationship-oriented. The debate has traditionally focused on whether a task or a relationship orientation creates better leadership, but in fact both are key to successfully leading a team. Typically, leaning more heavily on a task orientation at the outset of a project and shifting toward a relationship orientation once the work is in full swing works best.

7. Building on heritage relationships. When too many team members are strangers, people may be reluctant to share knowledge. The best practice is to put at least a few people who know one another on the team.

8. Understanding role clarity and task ambiguity. Cooperation increases when the roles of individual team members are sharply defined yet the team is given latitude on how to achieve the task.

Executive Support

At the most basic level, a team's success or failure at collaborating reflects the philosophy of top executives in the organization. Teams do well when executives invest in supporting social relationships, demonstrate collaborative behavior themselves, and create what we call a "gift culture"—one in which employees experience interactions with leaders and colleagues as something valuable and generously offered, a gift.

Investing in signature relationship practices.

When we looked at complex collaborative teams that were performing in a productive and innovative manner, we found that in every case the company's top executives had invested significantly in building and maintaining social relationships throughout the organization. However, the way they did that varied widely. The most collaborative companies had what we call "signature" practices—practices that were memorable, difficult for others to replicate, and particularly well suited to their own business environment.

For example, when Royal Bank of Scotland's CEO, Fred Goodwin, invested £350 million to open a new headquarters building outside Edinburgh in 2005, one of his goals was to foster productive collaboration among employees. Built around an indoor atrium, the new structure allows more than 3,000 people from the firm to rub shoulders daily.

The headquarters is designed to improve communication, increase the exchange of ideas, and create a sense of community among employees. Many of the offices have an open layout and look over the atrium—a vast transparent space. The campus is set up like a small town, with retail shops, restaurants, jogging tracks and cycling trails, spaces for picnics and barbecues—even a leisure club complete with swimming pool, gym, dance studios, tennis courts, and football pitches. The idea is that with a private "Main Street" running through the headquarters, employees will remain on the campus throughout the day—and be out of their offices mingling with colleagues for at least a portion of it.

To ensure that non-headquarters staff members feel they are a part of the action, Goodwin also commissioned an adjoining business school, where employees from other locations meet and learn. The visitors are encouraged to spend time on the headquarters campus and at forums designed to give employees opportunities to build relationships.

Indeed, the RBS teams we studied had very strong social relationships, a solid basis for collaborative activity that allowed them to accomplish tasks quickly. Take the Group Business Improvement (GBI) teams, which work on 30-, 60-, or 90-day projects ranging from back-office fixes to IT updates and are made up of people from across RBS's many businesses, including insurance, retail banking, and private banking in Europe and the United States. When RBS bought NatWest and migrated the new acquisition's technology platform to RBS's, the speed and success of the GBI teams confounded many market analysts.

BP has made another sort of signature investment. Because its employees are located all over the world, with relatively few at headquarters, the company aims to build social networks by moving employees across functions, businesses, and countries as part of their career development. When BP integrates an acquisition (it has grown by buying numerous smaller oil companies), the leadership development committee deliberately rotates employees from the acquired firm through positions across the corporation. Though the easier and cheaper call would be to leave the executives in their own units—where, after all, they know the business—BP instead trains them to take on new roles. As a consequence any senior team today is likely to be made up of people from multiple heritages. Changing roles frequently— it would not be uncommon for a senior leader at BP to have worked in four businesses and three geographic locations over the past decade—forces executives to become very good at meeting new people and building relationships with them.

Modeling collaborative behavior.

In companies with many thousands of employees, relatively few have the opportunity to observe the behavior of the senior team on a day-to-day basis. Nonetheless, we found that the perceived behavior of senior executives plays a significant role in determining how cooperative teams are prepared to be.

Executives at Standard Chartered Bank are exceptionally good role models when it comes to cooperation, a strength that many attribute to the firm's global trading heritage. The

Chartered Bank received its remit from Queen Victoria in 1853. The bank's traditional business was in cotton from Bombay (now Mumbai), indigo and tea from Calcutta, rice from Burma, sugar from Java, tobacco from Sumatra, hemp from Manila, and silk from Yokohama. The Standard Bank was founded in the Cape Province of South Africa in 1863 and was prominent in financing the development of the diamond fields and later gold mines. Standard Chartered was formed in 1969 through a merger of the two banks, and today the firm has 57 operating groups in 57 countries, with no home market.

It's widely accepted at Standard Chartered that members of the general management committee will frequently serve as substitutes for one another. The executives all know and understand the entire business and can fill in for each other easily on almost any task, whether it's leading a regional celebration, representing the company at a key external event, or kicking off an internal dialogue with employees.

While the behavior of the executive team is crucial to supporting a culture of collaboration, the challenge is to make executives' behavior visible. At Standard Chartered the senior team travels extensively; the norm is to travel even for relatively brief meetings. This investment in face-to-face interaction creates many opportunities for people across the company to see the top executives in action. Internal communication is frequent and open, and, maybe most telling, every site around the world is filled with photos of groups of executives—country and functional leaders—working together.

The senior team's collaborative nature trickles down throughout the organization. Employees quickly learn that the best way to get things done is through informal networks. For example, when a major program was recently launched to introduce a new customer-facing technology, the team responsible had an almost uncanny ability to understand who the key stakeholders at each branch bank were and how best to approach them. The team members' first-name acquaintance with people across the company brought a sense of dynamism to their interactions.

Creating a "gift culture."

A third important role for executives is to ensure that mentoring and coaching become embedded in their own routine behavior—and throughout the company. We looked at both formal mentoring processes, with clear roles and responsibilities, and less formal processes, where mentoring was integrated into everyday activities. It turned out that while both types were important, the latter was more likely to increase collaborative behavior. Daily coaching helps establish a cooperative "gift culture" in place of a more transactional "tit-for-tat culture."

At Nokia informal mentoring begins as soon as someone steps into a new job. Typically, within a few days, the employee's manager will sit down and list all the people in the organization, no matter in what location, it would be useful for the employee to meet. This is a deeply ingrained cultural norm, which probably originated when Nokia was a smaller and simpler organization. The manager sits with the newcomer, just as her manager sat with her when she joined, and reviews what topics the newcomer should discuss with each person on the list and why establishing a relationship with him or her is important. It is then standard for the newcomer to actively set up meetings with the people on the list, even when it means traveling to other locations. The gift of time—in the form of hours spent on coaching and building networks—is seen as crucial to the collaborative culture at Nokia.

Focused HR Practices

So what about human resources? Is collaboration solely in the hands of the executive team? In our study we looked at the impact of a wide variety of HR practices, including selection, performance management, promotion, rewards, and training, as well as formally sponsored coaching and mentoring programs.

We found some surprises: for example, that the type of reward system—whether based on team or individual achievement, or tied explicitly to collaborative behavior or not—had no discernible effect on complex teams' productivity and innovation. Although most formal HR programs appeared to have limited impact, we found that two practices did improve team performance: training in skills related to collaborative behavior, and support for informal community building. Where collaboration was strong, the HR team had typically made a significant investment in one or both of those practices—often in ways that uniquely represented the company's culture and business strategy.

Ensuring the requisite skills.

Many of the factors that support collaboration relate to what we call the "container" of collaboration—the underlying culture and habits of the company or team. However, we found that some teams had a collaborative culture but were not skilled in the practice of collaboration itself. They were encouraged to cooperate, they wanted to cooperate, but they didn't know how to work together very well in teams.

Our study showed that a number of skills were crucial: appreciating others, being able to engage in purposeful conversations, productively and creatively resolving conflicts, and program management. By training employees in those areas, a company's human resources or corporate learning department can make an important difference in team performance.

In the research, PricewaterhouseCoopers emerged as having one of the strongest capabilities in productive collaboration. With responsibility for developing 140,000 employees in nearly 150 countries, PwC's training includes modules that address teamwork, emotional intelligence, networking, holding difficult conversations, coaching, corporate social responsibility, and communicating the firm's strategy and shared values. PwC also teaches employees how to influence others effectively and build healthy partnerships.

A number of other successful teams in our sample came from organizations that had a commitment to teaching employees relationship skills. Lehman Brothers' flagship program for its client-facing staff, for instance, is its training in selling and relationship management. The program is not about sales techniques but, rather, focuses on how Lehman values its clients and makes sure that every client has access to all the resources the firm has to offer. It is essentially a course on strategies for building collaborative partnerships with customers, emphasizing the importance of trust-based personal relationships.

Supporting a sense of community.

While a communal spirit can develop spontaneously, we discovered that HR can also play a critical role in cultivating it, by sponsoring group events and activities such as women's networks, cooking weekends, and tennis coaching, or creating policies and practices that encourage them.

At ABN Amro we studied effective change-management teams within the company's enterprise services function. These informal groups were responsible for projects associated with the implementation of new technology throughout the bank; one team, for instance, was charged with expanding online banking services. To succeed, the teams needed the involvement and expertise of different parts of the organization.

The ABN Amro teams rated the company's support for informal communities very positively. The firm makes the technology needed for long-distance collaboration readily available to groups of individuals with shared interests—for instance, in specific technologies or markets—who hold frequent web conferences and communicate actively online. The company also encourages employees that travel to a new location to arrange meetings with as many people as possible. As projects are completed, working groups disband but employees maintain networks of connections. These practices serve to build a strong community over time—one that sets the stage for success with future projects.

Committed investment in informal networks is also a central plank of the HR strategy at Marriott. Despite its size and global reach, Marriott remains a family business, and the chairman, Bill Marriott, makes a point of communicating that idea regularly to employees. He still tells stories of counting sticky nickels at night as a child—proceeds from the root-beer stand founded in downtown Washington, DC, by his mother and father.

Many of the firm's HR investments reinforce a friendly, family-like culture. Almost every communication reflects an element of staff appreciation. A range of "pop-up" events—spontaneous activities—create a sense of fun and community. For example, the cafeteria might roll back to the 1950s, hold a twist dance contest, and in doing so, recognize the anniversary of the company's first hotel opening. Bill Marriott's birthday might be celebrated with parties throughout the company, serving as an occasion to emphasize the firm's culture and values. The chairman recently began his own blog, which is popular with employees, in which he discusses everything from Marriott's efforts to become greener, to his favorite family vacation spots—themes intended to reinforce the idea that the company is a community.

The Right Team Leaders

In the groups that had high levels of collaborative behavior, the team leaders clearly made a significant difference. The question in our minds was how they actually achieved this. The answer, we saw, lay in their flexibility as managers.

Assigning leaders who are both task- and relationship-oriented.

There has been much debate among both academics and senior managers about the most appropriate style for leading teams. Some people have suggested that relationship-oriented leadership is most appropriate in complex teams, since people are more likely to share knowledge in an environment of trust and goodwill. Others have argued that a task orientation—the ability to make objectives clear, to create a shared awareness of the dimensions of the task, and to provide monitoring and feedback—is most important.

How Complex Is the Collaborative Task?

Not all highly collaborative tasks are complex. In assembling and managing a team, consider the project you need to assign and whether the following statements apply:

- The task is unlikely to be accomplished successfully using only the skills within the team.

- The task must be addressed by a new group formed specifically for this purpose.

- The task requires collective input from highly specialized individuals.

- The task requires collective input and agreement from more than 20 people.

- The members of the team working on the task are in more than two locations.

- The success of the task is highly dependent on understanding preferences or needs of individuals outside the group.

- The outcome of the task will be influenced by events that are highly uncertain and difficult to predict.

- The task must be completed under extreme time pressure.

If more than two of these statements are true, the task requires complex collaboration.

In the 55 teams we studied, we found that the truth lay somewhere in between. The most productive, innovative teams were typically led by people who were *both* task- and relationship-oriented. What's more, these leaders changed their style during the project. Specifically, at the early stages they exhibited task-oriented leadership: They made the goal clear, engaged in debates about commitments, and clarified the responsibilities of individual team members. However, at a certain point in the development of the project they switched to a relationship orientation. This shift often took place once team members had nailed down the goals and their accountabilities and when the initial tensions around sharing knowledge had begun to emerge. An emphasis throughout a project on one style at the expense of the other inevitably hindered the long-term performance of the team, we found.

The most productive, innovative teams were led by people who were *both* task- and relationship-oriented. What's more, these leaders changed their style during the project..

Producing ambidextrous team leaders—those with both relationship and task skills—is a core goal of team-leadership development at Marriott. The company's performance-review process emphasizes growth in both kinds of skills. As evidence of their relationship skills, managers are asked to describe their peer network and cite examples of specific ways that network helped them succeed. They also must provide examples of how they've used relationship building to get things done. The development plans that follow these conversations explicitly map out how the managers can improve specific elements of their social relationships and networks. Such a plan might include, for instance, having lunch regularly with people from a particular community of interest.

To improve their task leadership, many people in the teams at Marriott participated in project-management certification programs, taking refresher courses to maintain their skills over time. Evidence of both kinds of capabilities becomes a significant criterion on which people are selected for key leadership roles at the company.

Team Formation and Structure

The final set of lessons for developing and managing complex teams has to do with the makeup and structure of the teams themselves.

Building on heritage relationships.

Given how important trust is to successful collaboration, forming teams that capitalize on preexisting, or "heritage," relationships, increases the chances of a project's success. Our research shows that new teams, particularly those with a high proportion of members who were strangers at the time of formation, find it more difficult to collaborate than those with established relationships.

Newly formed teams are forced to invest significant time and effort in building trusting relationships. However, when some team members already know and trust one another, they can become nodes, which over time evolve into networks. Looking closely at our data, we discovered that when 20% to 40% of the team members were already well connected to one another, the team had strong collaboration right from the start.

It helps, of course, if the company leadership has taken other measures to cultivate networks that cross boundaries. The orientation process at Nokia ensures that a large number of people on any team know one another, increasing the odds that even in a company of more than 100,000 people, someone on a companywide team knows someone else and can make introductions.

Nokia has also developed an organizational architecture designed to make good use of heritage relationships. When it needs to transfer skills across business functions or units, Nokia moves entire small teams intact instead of reshuffling individual people into new positions. If, for example, the company needs to bring together a group of market and technology experts to address a new customer need, the group formed would be composed of small pods of colleagues from each area. This ensures that key heritage relationships continue to strengthen over time, even as the organization redirects its resources to meet market needs. Because the entire company has one common platform for logistics, HR, finance, and other transactions, teams can switch in and out of businesses and geographies without learning new systems.

One important caveat about heritage relationships: If not skillfully managed, too many of them can actually disrupt collaboration. When a significant number of people within the team know one another, they tend to form strong subgroups—whether by function, geography, or anything else they have in common. When that happens, the probability of conflict among the subgroups, which we call fault lines, increases.

Understanding role clarity and task ambiguity.

Which is more important to promoting collaboration: a clearly defined approach toward achieving the goal, or clearly specified roles for individual team members? The common assumption is that carefully spelling out the approach is essential, but leaving the roles of individuals within the team vague will encourage people to share ideas and contribute in multiple dimensions.

Our research shows that the opposite is true: Collaboration improves when the roles of individual team members are clearly defined and well understood when individuals feel that they can do a significant portion of their work independently. Without such clarity, team members are likely to waste too much energy negotiating roles or protecting turf, rather than focus on the task. In addition, team members are more likely to want to collaborate if the path to achieving the team's goal is left somewhat ambiguous. If a team perceives the task as one that requires creativity, where the approach is not yet well known or predefined, its members are more likely to invest time and energy in collaboration.

At the BBC we studied the teams responsible for the radio and television broadcasts of the 2006 Proms (a two-month-long musical celebration), the team that televised the 2006 World Cup, and a team responsible for daytime television news. These teams were large—133 people worked on the Proms, 66 on the World Cup, and 72 on the news—and included members with a wide range of skills and from many disciplines. One would imagine, therefore, that there was a strong possibility of confusion among team members.

To the contrary, we found that the BBC's teams scored among the highest in our sample with regard to the clarity with which members viewed their own roles and the roles of others. Every team was composed of specialists who had deep expertise in their given function, and each person had a clearly defined role. There was little overlap between the responsibilities of the sound technician and the camera operator, and so on. Yet the tasks the BBC teams tackle are, by their very nature, uncertain, particularly when they involve breaking news. The trick the BBC has pulled off has been to clarify team members' individual roles with so much precision that it keeps friction to a minimum.

The successful teams we studied at Reuters worked out of far-flung locations, and often the team members didn't speak a common language. (The primary languages were Russian, Chinese, Thai, and English.) These teams, largely composed of software programmers, were responsible for the rapid development of highly complex technical software and network products. Many of the programmers sat at their desks for 12 hours straight developing code, speaking with no one. Ironically, these teams judged cooperative behavior to be high among their members. That may be because each individual was given autonomy over one discrete piece of the project. The rapid pace and demanding project timelines encouraged individual members to work independently to get the job done, but each person's work had to be shaped with an eye toward the overall team goal.

Strengthening your organization's capacity for collaboration requires a combination of long-term investments—in building relationships and trust, in developing a culture in which senior leaders are role models of cooperation—and smart near-term decisions about the ways teams are formed, roles are defined, and challenges and tasks are articulated. Practices and structures that may have worked well with simple teams of people who were all in one location and knew one another are likely to lead to failure when teams grow more complex.

Most of the factors that impede collaboration today would have impeded collaboration at any time in history. Yesterday's teams, however, didn't require the same amount of members, diversity, long-distance cooperation, or expertise that teams now need to solve global business challenges. So the models for teams need to be realigned with the demands of the current business environment. Through careful attention to the factors we've described in this article, companies can assemble the breadth of expertise needed to solve complex business problems—without inducing the destructive behaviors that can accompany it.

The Idea in Brief

To execute major initiatives in your organization—integrating a newly acquired firm, overhauling an IT system—you need **complex** teams. Such teams' defining characteristics—large, virtual, diverse, and specialized—are crucial for handling daunting projects. Yet these very characteristics can also destroy team members' ability to work together, say Gratton and Erickson. For instance, as team size grows, collaboration diminishes.

To maximize your complex teams' effectiveness, construct a basis for collaboration in your company. Eight practices hinging on relationship building and cultural change can help. For example, create a strong sense of community by sponsoring events and activities that bring people together and help them get to know one another. And use informal mentoring and coaching to encourage employees to view interaction with leaders and colleagues as valuable.

When executives, HR professionals, and team leaders all pitch in to apply these practices, complex teams hit the ground running—the day they're formed.

The Idea in Practice. The authors recommend these practices for encouraging collaboration in complex teams:

What Executives Can Do

- Invest in building and maintaining social relationships throughout your organization.

Example: Royal Bank of Scotland's CEO commissioned new headquarters built around an indoor atrium and featuring a "Main Street" with shops, picnic spaces, and a leisure club. The design encourages employees to rub shoulders daily, which fuels collaboration in RBS's complex teams.

- Model collaborative behavior.

Example: At Standard Chartered Bank, top executives frequently fill in for one another, whether leading regional celebrations, representing SCB at key external events, or initiating internal dialogues with employees. They make their collaborative behavior visible through extensive travel and photos of leaders from varied sites working together.

- Use coaching to reinforce a collaborative culture.

Example: At Nokia, each new hire's manager lists everyone in the organization the newcomer should meet, suggests topics he or she should discuss with each person on the list, and explains why establishing each of these relationships is important.

What HR Can Do

- Train employees in the specific skills required for collaboration: appreciating others, engaging in purposeful conversation, productively and creatively resolving conflicts, and managing programs.

- Support a sense of community by sponsoring events and activities such as networking groups, cooking weekends, or tennis coaching. Spontaneous, unannounced activities can further foster community spirit.

Example: Marriott has recognized the anniversary of the company's first hotel opening by rolling back the cafeteria to the 1950s and sponsoring a team twist dance contest.

What Team Leaders Can Do

- Ensure that at least 20%–40% of a new team's members already know one another.

Example: When Nokia needs to transfer skills across business functions or units, it moves entire small teams intact instead of reshuffling individual people into new positions.

- Change your leadership style as your team develops. At early stages in the project, be task-oriented: articulate the team's goal and accountabilities. As inevitable conflicts start emerging, switch to relationship building.

- Assign distinct roles so team members can do their work independently. They'll spend less time negotiating responsibilities or protecting turf. But leave the *path*

- to achieving the team's goal somewhat ambiguous. Lacking well-defined tasks, members are more likely to invest time and energy collaborating.

CHAPTER 4
When Teams Can't Decide

Leadership teams that can't reach consensus wait for the CEO to make the final call—and often are disappointed by the outcome. Frisch calls this phenomenon the *dictator-by-default syndrome*. Many companies turn to team-building and communication exercises to try to fix the situation. But that won't work, the author argues, because the trouble is not with the people, it's with the decision-making process. Attempting to arrive at a collective preference on the basis of individual opinions is inherently problematic. Once leadership teams realize that voting-system mathematics are the culprit, they can stop wasting time on irrelevant psychological exercises and instead adopt practical measures designed to break the impasse.

They must begin by acknowledging the problem and understanding what causes it. When more than two options are on the table, the scene is set for the CEO to become a dictator by default. Even yes-or-no choices present difficulties, because they always include a third, implied alternative: "Neither of the above."

When the CEO and the team understand why they have trouble making decisions, they can adopt the following tactics to minimize dysfunction: Clearly articulate the desired outcome, generate a range of options for achieving it, test "fences" (which can be moved) and "walls" (which cannot), surface preferences early, state each option's pros and cons, and devise new options that preserve the best features of existing ones.

Teams using such tactics need to adhere to two ground rules. First, they must deliberate confidentially, because a secure climate for conversation allows members to float trial balloons and cut deals. And second, members must be given enough time to study their options and assess the counterarguments. Only then can they achieve genuine alignment.

Suppose a nine-person leadership team that wants to cut costs is weighing three options: (a) closing plants, (b) moving from a direct sales force to distributors, and (c) reducing benefits and pay. While any individual executive may be able to "rack and stack" her preferences, it's possible for a majority to be simultaneously found for each alternative. Five members might prefer "closing plants" to "moving sales to distributors" ($a > b$), and a different set of five might prefer "moving sales" to "reducing benefits and pay" ($b > c$). By the transitive property, "closing plants" should be preferred to "reducing benefits and pay" ($a > c$). But the paradox is that five members could rank "reducing benefits and pay" over "closing plants" ($c > a$). Instead of being transitive, the preferences are circular.

When the CEO is finally forced to choose an option, only a minority of team members will agree with the decision. No matter which option is selected, it's likely that different majorities will prefer alternative outcomes. Moreover, as Arrow demonstrated, no voting method—not allocation of points to alternatives, not rank-ordering of choices, nothing—can solve the problem. It can be circumvented but not cured.

Although the concept is well understood in political science and economics and among some organizational theorists, it hasn't yet crossed over to practical management. Understanding this paradox could greatly alter the way executive teams make decisions.

1. Acknowledging the Problem

To circumvent the dictator-by-default syndrome, CEOs and their teams must first understand the conditions that give rise to it. The syndrome is perhaps most obvious at executive off-sites, but it can crop up in any executive committee meeting of substance.

Most executive teams are, in effect, legislatures. With the exception of the CEO, each member represents a significant constituency in the organization, from marketing to operations to finance. No matter how many times a CEO asks team members to take off their functional hats and view the organization holistically, the executives find it difficult to divorce themselves from their functional responsibilities. Because the team often focuses on assigning resources and setting priorities, members vie for allocations and approval for favored projects. When more than two options are on the table, the scene is set for the CEO to become a dictator by default.

More insidiously, the problem exists even when a team is considering an either/or choice, despite the fact that the voting paradox requires three or more options. Framing strategy considerations as binary choices—"We must either aggressively enter this market or get out of this line of business altogether"—appears to avert the problem. However, such choices always include a third, implied alternative: "Neither of the above." In other words, there could be circular majorities for entering the market, for exiting the business, and for doing neither.

Take, for example, the ubiquitous business case, which usually offers a single, affirmative recommendation: "We should aggressively enter this market now." The only apparent alternative is to forgo the market—but some team members may want to enter it more tentatively, others may want to enter an adjacent market, and still others may want to defer the decision until the market potential becomes clearer.

The use of the business case, which forces decisions into a yes-or-no framework, is a tacit admission that groups are not good at discussing and prioritizing multiple options. Further, when a team of analysts has spent six months working up the business case and only a half hour has been allotted to the item on the agenda, dissenting team members may be reluctant to speak up. Questions from the heads of sales and marketing, who have spent only a day or two with a briefing book and 20 minutes watching a PowerPoint presentation, would most likely be treated as comments tossed from the peanut gallery. So the team remains silent and unwittingly locked in the voting paradox. Ultimately, in order to move on to the next agenda item, either the team appears to reach a majority view or the CEO issues a fiat. In reality, however, there may be competing opinions, alternative majority opinions, and dissatisfaction with the outcome—all of them unstated.

2. Managing the Impossible

Once CEOs and their teams understand why they have trouble making decisions, they can adopt some straightforward tactics to minimize potential dysfunction.

Articulate clearly what outcome you are seeking.

It's surprising how often executives assume that they are talking about the same thing when in fact they are talking past one another. In a discussion of growth, for instance, some may be referring to revenue, others to market share, and others to net income. The discussion should begin with agreement on what outcome the team is trying to achieve. If it's growth, then do all the members agree on which measures are most relevant?

In the absence of clearly articulated goals, participants will choose options based on unspoken, often widely differing, premises, creating a situation that is ripe for the dictator-by-default syndrome. One division of a major industrial company, for example, was running out of manufacturing capacity for a commodity product made in the United States and a specialty product made in Western Europe. Because costs of labor and raw materials were high in both places, the leadership team was considering what seemed like an obvious choice: shutting down the U.S. plant and building a plant in China, where costs were lower and raw materials were closer, to handle the commodity business and any growth in the specialty business. Most members of the team assumed that the desired outcome was to achieve the highest possible return on net assets, which the move to China might well have accomplished.

However, the CEO had been in discussions with corporate managers who were primarily concerned with allocation of overhead throughout the enterprise. The move to China would mean shutting down an additional plant that supplied raw materials to the U.S. plant, with implications for corporate earnings. Once the division team fully understood what outcome the parent company desired—to minimize overhead costs without taking a hit on earnings— it could work on solving the capacity problem in a way that honored the parent's strictures.

It's essential to keep discussion of the desired outcome distinct from discussion about how to achieve it.

It's essential to keep discussion of the desired outcome distinct from discussion about how to achieve it. Sometimes, simply articulating the desired outcome will forestall or dissolve disagreement about solutions because the options can be tested against an accepted premise. It may also help avert the political horse trading that can occur when executives try to protect their interests rather than aiming for a common goal.

Provide a range of options for achieving outcomes.

Once the team at the industrial company had articulated the desired outcome, it could break the simplistic "accept," "reject," and "defer" alternatives into a more nuanced range of options: build a specialty plant in China; beef up the plant in Western Europe; or build a commodity plant in China and gradually decommission the U.S. plant.

Test fences and walls.

When teams are invited to think about options, they almost immediately focus on what they *can't* do—especially at the divisional level, where they may feel hemmed in by corporate policies, real or imagined. Often the entire team not only assumes that a constraint is real but also shies away when the discussion comes anywhere near it. When team members cite a presumed boundary, my colleagues and I encourage them to ask whether it's a wall, which can't be moved, or a fence, which can.

For example, one division of a global provider of financial services was looking at new avenues for growth. Although expanding the division's offerings to include banking services was a promising possibility, the executive team never considered it, assuming that corporate policy prohibited the company from entering banking. When the division head explicitly tested that assumption with her boss, she found that the real prohibition—the wall—was against doing anything that would bring certain types of new regulatory requirements. With that knowledge, the division's executive team was able to develop strategic options that included some features of banking but avoided any new regulations.

Surface preferences early.

Like juries, executive teams can get an initial sense of where they stand by taking nonbinding votes early in the discussion. They can also conduct surveys in advance of meetings in order to identify areas of agreement and disagreement as well as the potential for deadlock.

A global credit card company was deciding where to invest in growth. Ordinarily, executive team members would have embarked on an open-ended discussion in which numerous countries would be under consideration; that tactic would have invited the possibility of multiple majorities. Instead, they conducted a straw poll, quickly eliminating the countries that attracted no votes and focusing their subsequent discussion on the two places where there was the most agreement.

Using weighted preferences is another way to narrow the decision-making field and help prevent the dictator-by-default syndrome. The life and annuities division of a major insurance company had developed a business plan that included a growth in profit of $360 million. The executive team was trying to determine which line of business would deliver that growth. Instead of casting equally weighted votes for various lines of business, each executive was given poker chips representing $360 million and a grid with squares representing the company's products and channels. Team members distributed their chips according to where they thought the projected growth was likely to be found. After discussing the results they repeated the exercise, finding that some agreement emerged.

Proposing options early and allowing people to tailor them reduces the likelihood of a stalemate.

By the third and final round of the exercise, this weighted voting had helped them narrow their discussion to a handful of businesses and channels, and genuine alignment began to develop among team members. Equally weighted votes might have locked the executive team into the voting paradox, but this technique dissolved the false equality of alternatives that is often at the root of the problem. Proposing options early and allowing people to tailor them reduces the likelihood that executives will be forced into a stalemate that the CEO has to break.

State each option's pros and cons.

Rather than engaging in exercises about giving feedback or learning how to have assertive conversations, executives can better spend their time making sure that both sides of every option are forcefully voiced. That may require a devil's advocate.

The concept of a devil's advocate originated in the Roman Catholic Church's canonization process, in which a lawyer is appointed to argue against the canonization of a candidate—even the most apparently saintly. Similarly, in law, each side files its own brief; the defense doesn't simply respond off-the-cuff to the plaintiff's argument.

In business, however, an advocate for a particular option typically delivers a presentation that may contain some discussion of risk but remains entirely the work of someone who is sold on the idea. Members of the executive team are expected to agree with the business case or attack it, although they may have seen it only a few days before the meeting and thus have no way of producing an equally detailed rebuttal or offering solid alternatives. Further, attacking the business case is often perceived as attacking the person who is presenting it. Frequently the only executives with open license to ask tough, probing questions are the CEO and the CFO, but even they lack the detailed knowledge of the team advocating the business case.

By breaking the false binary of a business case into several explicit and implicit alternatives and assigning a devil's advocate to critique each option, you can depersonalize the discussion, making thorough and dispassionate counterarguments an expected part of strategic deliberations. This approach is especially valuable when the preferences of the CEO or other powerful members of the team are well known. If assigning a devil's advocate to each option appears too cumbersome, try a simpler variant: Have the CEO or a meeting facilitator urge each team member to offer two or three suggestions from the perspective of his functional area. Instead of unreasonably asking executives to think like a CEO, which usually elicits silence or perfunctory comments, this tactic puts team members on the solid ground of their expertise and transforms an unsatisfying false binary into far more options for discussion.

A major internet entertainment company adopted a novel version of the devil's advocate approach. The company maintains a council to consider its many potential investments, from upgrading its server farms to adopting new technology to creating special entertainment events on the web. In the past, each opportunity was presented to the council as a business case by an advocate of the investment, and each case was evaluated in isolation.

Frustrated with this haphazard approach, the company established a new system: The council now considers all investment proposals as a portfolio at its monthly strategy meetings. All proposals follow an identical template, allowing for easy comparison and a uniform scoring system. Finally, each one needs sign-off from an independent executive.

This system incorporates the devil's advocate role at two levels. For each proposal the validating executive, not wishing to be accountable for groundless optimism, considers carefully all of the counterarguments, does a reality check, and makes sure the sponsor adjusts the score accordingly. At the portfolio level, the comparative-scoring system reminds the team that the proposals are competing for limited resources, which prompts a more critical assessment.

Devise new options that preserve the best features of existing ones.

Despite a team's best efforts, executives can still find themselves at an impasse. That is a measure of both the weightiness of some strategic decisions and the intractability of the voting paradox—it's not necessarily an index of executive dysfunction.

Teams should continue to reframe their options in ways that preserve their original intent, be it a higher return on net assets or greater growth. When they feel the impulse to shoehorn decisions into an either/or framework, they should step back and generate a broader range of options. For instance, the executive team of the property and casualty division of a large insurer wanted to grow either by significantly increasing the company's share with existing agencies or by increasing the total number of agencies that sold its products. Before the leadership team took either path, it needed to decide whether to offer a full line of products or a narrow line. As a result, team members found themselves considering four business models: (1) full product line, existing large agencies; (2) narrow product line, existing large agencies; (3) full product line, more small agencies; and (4) narrow product line, more small agencies. Dissatisfied with those choices, they broke the business down into 16 value attributes, including brand, claim service, agency compensation, price competitiveness, breadth of product offering, and agency-facing technology. Some of these value attributes might apply to all four of the original business models; others to three or fewer. Agent-facing technology, for example, is typical of working with many small agencies, because their sheer numbers preclude high-touch relationships with each one.

The team then graded its company and several competitors on each attribute to find competitive openings that fit with the division's willingness and ability to invest. Instead of four static choices, it now had a much larger number of choices based on different combinations of value attributes. Ultimately, it chose to bring several lagging attributes up to market standard, elevate others to above-market standard, and aggressively emphasize still others. This turned out to be a far less radical redirection than the team had originally assumed was needed.

3.   Two Essential Ground Rules

So far, I have outlined several tactics that leadership teams can use to circumvent the dictator-by-default syndrome. These tactics can be effective whether they are used singly or in tandem. But if teams are to thwart this syndrome, they must adhere to two ground rules.

Deliberate confidentially.

A secure climate for the conversation is essential to allow team members to float trial balloons and cut deals. An executive who knows that her speculative remarks about closing plants may be circulated throughout the company will be reluctant to engage in the free play of mind that unfettered strategy discussion demands. Moreover, team members whose priorities don't prevail in the deliberations must be able to save face when the meeting is over. If they are known to have "lost" or to have relinquished something dear to their constituents, their future effectiveness as leaders might be undermined.

Deliberate over an appropriate time frame.

All too often the agendas for strategy off-sites contain items like "China market strategy," with 45 minutes allotted for the decision. The result is a discussion that goes nowhere or an arbitrary decision by the CEO that runs roughshod over competing majorities for other options. When new options are devised or existing ones unbundled, team members need time to study them carefully and assess the counterarguments. Breaking up the discussion into several meetings spaced widely apart and interspersed with additional analysis and research gives people a chance to reconsider their preferences. It also gives them time to prepare their constituencies for changes that are likely to emerge as a result of a new strategy.

Leadership and communication exercises have their merits. A team can't make effective decisions if its members don't trust one another or if they fail to listen to one another. The problem I see most often, however, is one that simply cannot be fixed with the psychological tools so often touted in management literature. If executives employ the tactics described here, which are designed to fix the decision-making process, they will have far greater success in achieving real alignment.

The Idea in Brief

When cross-functional teams have trouble making decisions, leaders blame psychological factors like mistrust or poor communication. But the problem isn't the team's people; it's the decision-making process. Each member has constituencies in the organization. So each vies for resources for favored projects—virtually guaranteeing an impasse. To break the impasse, the team leader makes a unilateral decision, leaving a majority of the team disgruntled and resentful of the "dictator."

To improve your team's decision-making process, Frisch recommends several tactics. For example, clearly articulate the outcome your team must achieve. When people understand the goal, they more readily agree on how to get there. And surface members' functional preferences through pre-meeting surveys to identify areas of agreement and disagreement and to gauge the potential for deadlock.

These deceptively simple tactics position your team to prevent stalemates instead of forcing you to be "dictator-by-default."

The Idea in Practice. Frisch suggests these tactics for improving your team's decision-making process:

1. Specify the Desired Outcome

Without clear desired outcomes, team members choose options based on unspoken, differing assumptions. This sets the stage for the dictator-by-default syndrome. To avoid the syndrome, articulate what you want the team to accomplish. Example:

A division of an industrial company was running out of manufacturing capacity for a product made in the U.S. The leadership team assumed the desired outcome was "Achieve the highest possible return on assets." So they discussed shuttering a U.S. plant and building a plant in China, where costs were lower and raw materials closer. But the parent company's desired outcome was "Minimize corporate overhead and maximize earnings." The move to China would mean closing an additional facility that supplied materials to the U.S. plant, significantly lowering earnings. Once the division team understood the desired outcome, it could solve the capacity problem in a way that was consistent with the parent's actual goals.

2. Provide a Range of Options for Achieving the Desired Outcome

Break alternatives into a broader range of options beyond "Accept the proposed plan," "Reject the plan," and "Defer the decision."

3.   Test Fences and Walls

When team members cite a presumed boundary (for example, a real or imagined corporate policy), ask "Is it a wall (it's relatively immovable) or is it a fence (it can be moved)?" Example:

For a division of a global financial services provider, executives never considered expanding their offerings to include banking services. That's because they thought corporate policy prohibited entry into banking. When the division head tested this assumption with her boss, she learned that the real concern was not to do anything that would bring new regulatory requirements (the wall). So the division developed strategic options that included several features of banking that avoided dealing with new regulations.

4.   Surface Preferences Early

Survey members before meetings to identify their preferences and focus the subsequent discussion. Example:

A global credit card company was deciding where to invest in growth. Executive team members conducted a straw poll of countries under consideration. The process enabled them to quickly eliminate countries that attracted no votes. And it focused their subsequent discussion on the two regions where there was most agreement.

5.   Assign Devil's Advocates

Make thorough and dispassionate counterarguments an expected part of strategic deliberations. Assign devil's advocates to make the case against each option. This depersonalizes the discussion and produces more nuanced strategy discussions.

The executive team is deliberating about a critical strategic choice, but no matter how much time and effort the team members expend, they cannot reach a satisfactory decision. Then comes that uncomfortable moment when all eyes turn to the CEO. The team waits for the boss to make the final call, yet when it's made, few people like the decision. Blame, though unspoken, is plentiful. The CEO blames the executives for indecisiveness; they resent the CEO for acting like a dictator. If this sounds familiar, you've experienced what I call the *dictator-by-default syndrome.*

For decades this dynamic has been diagnosed as a problem of leadership or teamwork or both. To combat it, companies use team-building and communications exercises that teach executives how to have assertive conversations, give and receive feedback, and establish mutual trust. In doing so, they miss the real problem, which lies not with the people but with the process. This sort of impasse is inherent in the act of arriving at a collective preference on the basis of individual preferences. Once leadership teams understand that voting-system mathematics are the culprit, they can stop wasting time on irrelevant psychological exercises and instead adopt practical measures designed to break the impasse. These measures, proven effective in scores of strategy off-sites for companies of all sizes, enable teams to move beyond the blame cycle to a no-fault style of decision making.

6.   Asking the Impossible

Reaching collective decisions based on individual preferences is an imperfect science. Majority wishes can clash when a group of three or more people attempts to set priorities among three or more items. This "voting paradox," first noted in the eighteenth century by the Marquis de Condorcet, a French mathematician and social theorist, arises because different subsets of the group can generate conflicting majorities for all possible alternatives. A century and a half later, renowned economist Ken Arrow developed his impossibility theorem, which established a series of mathematical proofs based on Condorcet's work.

CHAPTER 5

The Competitive Imperative of Learning

Most executives believe that relentless execution—efficient, timely, consistent production and delivery of goods or services—is the surefire path to customer satisfaction and positive financial results. But this is a myth in the knowledge economy, argues Edmondson, a Harvard Business School professor. She points to General Motors, which for years has remained wedded to a well-developed competency in centralized controls and efficient execution but has steadily lost ground, posting a record $38.7 billion loss in 2007. Such an *execution-as-efficiency* model results in employees who are exceedingly reluctant to offer ideas or voice questions and concerns. Placing value only on getting things right the first time, organizations are unable to take the risks necessary to improve and evolve.

By contrast, firms that put a premium on what Edmondson calls *execution-as-learning* focus not so much on how a process should be carried out as on how it should evolve. Since 1980 General Electric, for instance, has continued to reinvent itself in every field from wind energy to medical diagnostics; and it enjoyed a $22.5 billion profit in 2007.

Organizations that foster execution-as-learning provide employees with psychological safety. No one is penalized for asking for help or making a mistake. These companies also employ four distinct approaches to day-to-day work: They use the best available knowledge (which is understood to be a moving target) to inform the design of specific process guidelines. They encourage employee collaboration by making information available when and where it's needed. They routinely capture data on processes to discover how work really happens. Finally, they study these data in an effort to find ways to improve execution. Taken together, these practices form the basis of a learning infrastructure that makes continual learning part of business as usual.

Most executives believe that relentless execution—the efficient, timely, consistent production and delivery of goods or services—is the surefire path to customer satisfaction and financial results. Managers who let up on execution even briefly, the assumption goes, do so at their peril.

In fact, even flawless execution cannot guarantee enduring success in the knowledge economy. The influx of new knowledge in most fields makes it easy to fall behind. Consider General Motors—the largest, most profitable company in the world in the early 1970s. Confident of the wisdom of its approach, GM remained wedded to a well-developed competency in centralized control and high-volume execution. Despite this, the firm steadily lost ground in subsequent decades and posted a record $38.7 billion loss in 2007. Like many dominant companies in the industrial era, General Motors was slow to understand that great execution is difficult to sustain—not because people get tired of working hard, but because the managerial mind-set that enables efficient execution inhibits employees' ability to learn and innovate. A focus on getting things done, and done right, crowds out the experimentation and reflection vital to sustainable success.

A focus on getting things done, and done right, crowds out the experimentation and reflection vital to sustainable success.

My research identifies a different approach to execution—what I call *execution-as-learning*—that promotes success over the long haul. Think of General Electric, another powerhouse born in the industrial era. Since the 1980s, the company has constantly evaluated its activities, found ways to improve, and built the expectation that learning will be ongoing into management practices. As a result, GE has continued to reinvent itself with operations in every field from wind energy to medical diagnostics, and it posted a $22.5 billion profit in 2007.

Execution-as-**Efficiency** vs. Execution-as-**Learning**	
Leaders provide answers.	Leaders set direction and articulate the mission.
Employees follow directions.	Employees (usually in teams) discover answers.
Optimal work processes are designed and set up in advance.	Tentative work processes are set up as a starting point.
New work processes are developed infrequently; implementing change is a huge undertaking.	Work processes keep developing; small changes—experiments and improvements—are a way of life.
Feedback is typically one-way (from boss to employee) and corrective ("You're not doing it right.")	Feedback is always two-way: The boss gives feedback in the form of coaching and advice; team members give feedback about what they're learning from doing the (ever-changing) work.
Problem solving is rarely required; judgment is not expected; employees ask managers when they're unsure.	Problem solving is constantly needed, so valuable information is provided to guide employees' judgment.
Fear (of the boss or of consequences) is often part of the work environment and generally does not appreciably harm the quality of execution; it may even motivate effort and attentiveness in those facing an otherwise dull task.	Fear cripples the learning process: It inhibits experimentation, lowers awareness of options, and discourages people from sharing and analyzing insights, questions, and problems.

From a distance, execution-as-learning looks a lot like execution-as-efficiency. There's the same discipline, respect for systems, and attention to detail. Look closer, however, and you find a radically different organizational mind-set, one that focuses not so much on making sure a process is carried out as on helping it evolve, building four unique approaches into day-to-day work.

Execution-as-Efficiency vs. Execution-as-Learning Execution-as-EfficiencyLeaders provide answers.Employees follow directions.Optimal work processes are designed and set up in advance.New work processes are developed infrequently; implementing change is a huge undertaking.Feedback is typically one-way (from boss to employee) and corrective ("You're not doing it right.")Problem solving is rarely required; judgment is not expected; employees ask managers when they're unsure.Fear (of the boss or of consequences) is often part of the work environment and generally does not appreciably harm the quality of execution; it may even motivate effort and attentiveness in those facing an otherwise dull task.Execution-as-LearningLeaders set direction and articulate the mission.Employees (usually in teams) discover answers.Tentative work processes are set up as a starting point.Work processes keep developing; small changes—experiments and improvements—are a way of life.Feedback is always two-way: The boss gives feedback in the form of coaching and advice; team members give feedback about what they're learning from doing the (ever-changing) work.Problem solving is constantly needed, so valuable information is provided to guide employees' judgment.Fear cripples the learning process: It inhibits experimentation, lowers awareness of options, and discourages people from sharing and analyzing insights, questions, and problems.

First, organizations that focus on execution-as-learning use the best knowledge obtainable (which is understood to be a moving target) to inform the design of specific process guidelines. Second, they enable their employees to collaborate by making information available when and where it's needed. Third, they routinely capture process data to discover how work is really being done. Finally, they study these data in an effort to find ways to improve. These four practices form the basis of a learning infrastructure that runs through the fabric of the organization, making continual learning part of business as usual.

Having studied knowledge organizations—hospitals, in particular—for nearly 20 years, I'd like to offer a new definition of what successful execution looks like in the knowledge economy: The best organizations have figured out how to learn quickly while maintaining high quality standards.

What's Wrong with Execution?

Most management systems in use today date back to a manufacturing-dominated era in which firms were organized to execute as efficiently as possible. Throughout the twentieth century, the core challenge factory managers faced was controlling variability. In their approach to large-scale auto manufacturing, for example, pioneering thinkers like Henry Ford and Frederick Taylor sought to parcel out simple, repetitive tasks to people on an assembly line to reduce the likelihood of human error while producing as many cars as possible. Later, manufacturing managers adopted tools such as statistical process control to help make sure the job got done right, every time. For a long while and in many circumstances, management systems that were focused on execution-as-efficiency worked brilliantly, transforming unpredictable and expensive customized work into uniform, economical modes of mass production.

Underlying the notion of a simple, controllable production system was the notion of the simple, controllable employee. In the factory model of management, it was easy to monitor workers and measure their output. Because the work itself was not terribly interesting or motivating in its own right, managers intuitively relied on what Freud called "the pleasure principle," the idea that human beings are motivated to seek pleasure and avoid pain. Thus supervisors used a combination of carrots (more pay for more tasks completed) and sticks (reprimands or the threat of job loss) to motivate employees. These behavioral strategies were very successful, but they produced an unfortunate legacy that still characterizes many workplaces today—an undercurrent of fear.

With the rise of knowledge-based organizations in the information age, the old model no longer works, for a number of reasons. In such organizations, it's difficult, if not impossible, to monitor employee productivity or measure individual performance in simple ways, such as by hours worked. Performance is increasingly determined by factors that can't be overseen: intelligent experimentation, ingenuity, interpersonal skills, resilience in the face of adversity, for instance. Consider a hospital emergency room. At any moment, a patient with a previously unheard-of set of symptoms might walk in, and specialists from several departments—reception, nursing, medicine, laboratory, surgery, pharmacy—need to coordinate their efforts if the patient is to receive effective care. These people must resolve conflicting priorities and opinions quickly. As in most knowledge organizations, room to maneuver is extraordinarily high. People rely on their own and their colleagues' judgment and expertise, rather than on management direction, to decide what to do. When work is interdependent and in flux, as it is in this situation, interpersonal fear is not only unhelpful—it's downright counterproductive.

By continuing to think of execution in the old-fashioned, narrow sense, companies fall into predictable self-sabotaging traps:

Critical information and ideas fail to rise to the top.

When people get the message that speed, efficiency, and results are what matter, they become exceedingly reluctant to risk taking up managers' time with any but the most certain and positive of inputs. They don't offer ideas, concerns, or even questions. One study at a high-tech multinational found that over half the employees believed it was unsafe to say what was on their minds. Subsequent interviews revealed that employees withheld not only bad news but also new ideas; both seemed risky because of higher-ups' emphasis on superb and timely performance.

Consider the example of a team leader who tried to stimulate honest reflection about a large software-development project. He opened a post-project review by stating what he believed he himself could have done better. To his surprise, this honest self-assessment came back to haunt him when, during his next performance review, his manager noted, "I see you have made some mistakes this year," and used the data to lower his ratings. When employees feel they can't speak up about small failures, their organizations are at increased risk for large ones.

People don't have enough time to learn.

An exclusive focus on execution-as-efficiency leads companies to delay, discourage, or understaff investments in areas where learning is critical. It's a given that switching to a new approach can lower performance in the short run. The fastest hunt-and-peck typist must endure a short-term hit to performance while learning to touch-type, just as the tennis player suffers initially when shifting to a new, better serve. These are the costs of learning, which has its payoff in future performance. Managers who overemphasize results can subtly discourage technologies, skills, or practices that make new approaches viable.

When a major telecommunications firm launched the technologically new digital subscriber line (DSL) internet service in the late 1990s, it set ambitious production targets that failed to take the need for learning into account. The staff did not have sufficient time to work out how to implement new software and hardware that had to operate with customers' not always up-to-date personal computer equipment: The result was a customer service nightmare.

Unhealthy internal competition arises.

To motivate people to execute well, companies often reward those divisions or plants with the best performance. This can make people reluctant to share ideas or best practices with their colleagues in other groups. Following his successful turnaround of the Simmons Bedding Company in 2003, CEO Charlie Eitel said in an interview that the firm's 18 manufacturing plants—formerly competitors for a single annual award for best producer—had been individually hoarding successful practices for years. By adding incentives for absolute, rather than relative, quality and productivity, the company shifted its culture, encouraging people in different plants to share information—and saved $21 million through process improvements in the first year.

Companies think they can do no wrong.

When a successful business is wedded to its execution-as-efficiency approach, managers can fall prey to a classic attribution error: the conclusion that the company's success is evidence of its wisdom. General Motors' confidence in its centralized control systems blinded the company to major shifts in the automotive market, including customers' preference for smaller, fuel-efficient cars and the growing presence of foreign competitors in the U.S. market. Similarly, HBS professor Mary Tripsas has shown, Polaroid's confidence in its instant-film business model blocked senior executives' ability to appreciate the opportunities presented by digital imaging.

First, Make It Safe

While General Motors was placing its faith in its execution efficiencies, Toyota was taking a different route, focusing on bottom-up process improvements of much the sort we're discussing here, famously allowing any employee who saw a problem—small or large—to stop the line. Toyota has made no secret of its approach and invites executives the world over to come to its factories and see for themselves. And yet when visitors return to their own companies and try to put Toyota-like systems in place, many are disappointed, having failed to import the mind-set and culture that make the system work.

My research on why people withhold constructive ideas in the workplace suggests that before execution-as-learning can occur, organizations must fulfill one big prerequisite: They need to foster psychological safety. This means ensuring that no one is penalized if they ask for help or admit a mistake. Psychological safety is crucial, especially in organizations where knowledge constantly changes, where workers need to collaborate, and where those workers must make wise decisions without management intervention. It's built on the premise that no one can perform perfectly in every situation when knowledge and best practice are moving targets.

In her research on individual mind-set differences, Stanford psychologist Carol Dweck has shown that the way children view a task affects their persistence and performance over time. Some children think of human ability or intelligence as fixed and, consequently, think of school tasks as performance opportunities—moments of truth that prove whether or not they're smart. For these children, performing poorly on an assignment or a test would demonstrate that they lacked intelligence rather than indicating that they had more to learn. Believing that the point of execution is to demonstrate competence, they go out of their way to pick easier tasks. Of course, this means they lose out when it comes to learning. This same mind-set encourages managers to admire and expect to be rewarded for decisiveness, efficiency, and action rather than for reflection, inquiry, and collaboration, the uncertainty of which makes them uncomfortable. Like the children who have learned to shun new challenges, these managers avoid, and help others avoid, the risks of questions and experiments.

In psychologically safe environments, people are willing to offer up ideas, questions, concerns—they are even willing to fail—and when they do, they learn. In her studies, Dweck found that some children—those who early on were rewarded for effort and creativity more than for simply giving the right answer—see intelligence as something malleable that improves with attention and effort. Tasks are opportunities for learning; failure is just evidence that they haven't mastered the task yet. Driven by curiosity about what will and will not work, they experiment. When things don't pan out, they don't give up or see themselves as inadequate. They pay attention to what went wrong and try something different next time. In adults, such a mind-set allows managers to strike the right tone of openness, humility, curiosity, and humor in ways that encourage their teams to learn.

Some managers might argue that fostering psychological safety can make it difficult to hold people accountable. Certainly, if employees feel particularly close to one another and the managerial hand is relatively weak, performance standards can slip. But in general, psychological safety is independent from employee accountability, and healthy organizations foster both by setting high performance aspirations while acknowledging areas of uncertainty that require continued exploration or debate. Setting ambitious goals while conceding the limits of current knowledge encourages striving without shutting down inquiry. On the other hand, an undue focus on accountability without psychological safety can produce a variety of organizational dysfunctions. (For more on this, see the exhibit "Does Psychological Safety Hinder Performance?")

Does Psychological Safety Hinder Performance?

Psychological safety does not operate at the expense of employee accountability; the most effective organizations achieve high levels of both, as this matrix shows.

Psychological safety is not about being nice—or about lowering performance standards. Quite the opposite: It's about recognizing that high performance *requires* the openness, flexibility, and interdependence that can develop only in a psychologically safe environment, especially when the situation is changing or complex. Psychological safety makes it possible to give tough feedback and have difficult conversations—which demand trust and respect—without the need to tiptoe around the truth.

Not surprisingly, the most important influence on psychological safety is the nearest boss. Signals sent by people in power are critical to employees' ability and willingness to offer their ideas and observations. This means that levels of psychological safety vary strikingly from department to department and work group to work group, even in organizations known for having a powerful corporate culture. In a study of eight units in two teaching hospitals, for example, I found large differences in employees' beliefs about whether it was safe to report medication errors—and differences in error-reporting rates as high as tenfold. As a result, some units were identifying risks and coming up with ways to avoid future problems, while others were not because the people in them were terrified to speak up.

Accountability for Meeting Demanding Goals

	LOW	**HIGH**
Psychological Safety — HIGH	**Comfort zone** Employees really enjoy working with one another but don't feel particularly challenged. Nor do they work very hard. Some family businesses and small consultancies fall into this quadrant.	**Learning zone** Here the focus is on collaboration and learning in the service of high-performance outcomes. The hospitals described in this article fall into this quadrant.
Psychological Safety — LOW	**Apathy zone** Employees tend to be apathetic and spend their time jockeying for position. Typical organizations in this quadrant are large, top-heavy bureaucracies, where people fulfill their functions but the preferred modus operandi is to curry favor rather than to share ideas.	**Anxiety zone** Such firms are breeding grounds for anxiety. People fear to offer tentative ideas, try new things, or ask colleagues for help, even though they know great work requires all three. Some investment banks and high-powered consultancies fall into this quadrant.

Such findings shine the spotlight, for better or worse, on middle managers. How can they help create psychological safety in the groups they lead? A couple of simple, if not always intuitive, steps appear to make an enormous difference.

The first is to explicitly acknowledge the lack of answers to the tough problems groups face. (Strange as it may seem, very few managers do this. It's not that they don't recognize the imperfect state of knowledge; they just fail to mention it.) Acknowledging uncertainty may seem like a weakness, but in fact it's usually an intelligent and accurate diagnosis of a murky situation. When supervisors admit that they don't know something or made a mistake, their genuine display of humility encourages others to do the same.

The second is to ask questions—real questions, not leading or rhetorical ones. Simply put, when people believe that their managers want to hear from them and value their input, they respond more. Indeed, one could feel awkward or foolish not speaking in response to a question.

This is especially so when lives are on the line. In one study of quality-improvement projects in intensive-care units at 23 hospitals, my colleagues and I showed that when medical directors asked questions, acknowledged their own fallibility or lack of knowledge, and appreciated others' contributions, the people in their units felt a higher degree of psychological safety than those in units whose leaders did not do so. As a result, these units more quickly adopted new practices that could reduce infection rates and lead to other improvements in patient care.

Senior executives, too, play an important role in building psychological safety. For instance, as CEO of Prudential Financial, Art Ryan instituted a series of training initiatives called "Safe to Say" to let employees know that their voices were not only welcome but required for success. Eli Lilly's chief science officer introduced "failure parties" to honor intelligent experiments that failed. Policy interventions like these work best when accompanied by a clear and credible rationale for why openness and directness are needed to achieve superb performance. Senior executives may be best positioned to convey this message.

Execution-as-Learning: Four Steps

Organizations that adopt an execution-as-learning model don't focus on getting things done more efficiently than competitors do. Instead, they focus on learning faster. The goal is to find out what works and what doesn't; employees must absorb new knowledge while executing, often sacrificing short-term efficiency to gain insight into and respond to novel problems. My research has revealed four steps for making this happen.

Step 1: Provide process guidelines.

Figuring out the best ways to accomplish different kinds of work in a rapidly changing environment starts with seeking out best practices gathered from experts, publications, and even competitors. The path to execution-as-learning is thus similar to the path to efficiency—it starts with establishing standard processes. But the goal of these processes is not so much to produce efficiency as to facilitate learning, because effective knowledge organizations recognize that today's best practices won't be tomorrow's and won't work in every situation.

For example, the renowned design firm IDEO adheres faithfully to a standard process for developing its many innovative products. Similarly, in a hospital, even though each patient is unique, standard protocols make it easier for medical specialists to think in real time about the individual features of the case because the steps common to all patients with a particular condition are prescribed in advance. Standard processes both simplify routine action and highlight discrepancies in specific cases that suggest the need for process innovation or refinement.

To understand how this works, let's look at an extraordinary health care organization called Intermountain Healthcare (IHC), an integrated system of over 100 facilities—including 21 hospitals, and numerous health centers, outpatient clinics, counseling centers, and group practices—located across Utah and southeastern Idaho. To increase employees' chances of making good decisions under pressure and reduce unwanted variability in patient care, senior management put together 60 teams of experts on different diseases to develop detailed process guidelines for treating patients with those conditions. The high quality of these guidelines—designed to reflect the current best practices in the medical literature—was the result of analysis and debate by professionals in nursing and medicine who held diverse points of view. Each team worked hard to develop a set of clinical-care processes outlining the way patient care should unfold on the front lines. Similarly, Children's Hospitals and Clinics of Minnesota convenes teams to review and standardize different types of care, using principles of lean manufacturing.

Step 2: Provide tools that enable employees to collaborate in real time.

No matter how much thought goes into advance planning, knowledge work often requires people to make concurrent collaborative decisions in response to unforeseen, novel, or complex problems. That is why another leading medical center, the Cleveland Clinic, developed its own state-of-the-art information technology systems that enable dispersed individuals participating in a particular patient's care to work together virtually. Dr. Martin Harris, the clinic's chief information officer, explains that the IT infrastructure "connects every caregiver in all of our facilities throughout Ohio and Florida into what is essentially a single medical practice. That means that all the vital medical information related to each patient is available to any caregiver in our health system whenever and wherever it is needed." When a patient sees several physicians, as is often the case, caregivers working in different locations at different times can coordinate effectively. For example, through an automated alert function, physicians learn of drugs others have prescribed, thereby ensuring that medication decisions with interdependent consequences are made safely.

Fostering face-to-face collaboration is also critical in the knowledge economy. The most effective organizations I studied provided forums to build networks and training in team skills, both of which bring critical areas of expertise and responsibility together. For example, Groupe Danone, the global food company, uses knowledge "marketplaces"—lively events that occur during company conferences—to encourage frontline managers to share best practices and to innovate by suggesting new processes and products. Simmons Bedding developed an extensive training system to develop employees' team skills, which helps them build relationships that foster collaboration within and across all of its plants.

Step 3: Collect process data.

Execution-as-efficiency focuses on performance data, which capture what happened. Execution-as-learning pays just as much attention to process data, which describe how work unfolds. IHC, for example, recognized that physicians, as highly educated experts, might resist process guidelines developed by a committee. For that reason and others, IHC does not discourage doctors from deviating from the guidelines. In fact, the organization *invites* them to, anytime they judge that good patient care requires it. The only condition: They have to help IHC learn by entering into the computer what they did differently—and why. This valuable feedback is captured in the system and periodically used by the expert teams to make updates or refinements. Most of the time, the deviations help identify ways the guidelines could be made more precise by taking relevant patient differences into account. The fact that protocols are not hard-and-fast rules but are instead flexible made them acceptable to physicians. Likewise, the Cleveland Clinic created a formal Quality Institute to standardize measures and supervise the collection and analysis of both process and outcome data to help identify and then spread best practices. At Minnesota Children's Hospitals, data on both adverse events and close calls are captured as inputs to the next stage of the learning process.

Step 4: Institutionalize disciplined reflection.

The goal of collecting process data is to understand what goes right and what goes wrong, and to prevent failures from recurring. At IHC, teams of experts periodically analyze data collected during clinical activities. Often, these analyses suggest improvements to the guidelines, which are then integrated into the design of future processes. At the Cleveland Clinic, teams of physicians drawn from hospitals all over the system study process data and identify areas for improvement throughout the organization's many sites. By 2006, the Clinic had seven such teams, including heart failure, stroke, diabetes, and orthopedic surgery. Process data showed, for instance, that stroke patients treated at various sites at the Clinic had not always received a blood thinner within the three-hour window that research identified as the standard of care. An analysis of patient outcomes helped to make the blood-thinner treatment the standard of stroke care for all Cleveland Clinic hospitals. As a result of this disciplined reflection, the hospitals doubled their use of the blood thinner and reduced complications from stroke by 50%. Similarly, at Children's, unit-based safety action teams meet regularly to reflect on what they are learning about identifying hazards that can pose risks to their vulnerable young patients.

It's not easy for a hospital, or any other organization facing cost constraints, to do this. Disciplined reflection takes productive resources off-line, and conventional management wisdom can't help but see this as lost productivity. Nonetheless, the only way to achieve and sustain excellence is for leaders to insist that their organizations invest in the slack time and resources that support this step.

I do not mean to imply that old-style execution-as-efficiency must always go by the wayside. Obviously, there are workplaces—call centers, fast-food restaurants, manufacturing plants— where doing things better and faster than the competition is critical. But even in such organizations, employees must learn if they are to improve. In work environments characterized by fear, the four steps described above become difficult, if not impossible, to follow.

When people know their ideas are welcome, they will offer innovative ways to lower costs.

Fostering an atmosphere in which trust and respect thrive, and flexibility and innovation flourish, pays off in most settings, even the most deadline driven. When managers empower, rather than control; when they ask the right questions, rather than provide the right answers; and when they focus on flexibility, rather than insist on adherence, they move to a higher form of execution. And when people know their ideas are welcome, they will offer innovative ways to lower costs and improve quality—thus laying a more solid foundation for their organization's success.

The Idea in Brief

Most managers believe that relentless execution—the efficient, timely production and delivery of offerings—is vital to corporate performance. Execution-as-efficiency is important. But focusing *too* narrowly on it can prevent your company from adapting effectively to change.

Consider General Motors: Managers' confidence in GM's famously efficient control systems blinded them to big shifts in the market, including customers' preferences for fuel-efficient cars. GM posted a $38.7 billion loss in 2007.

Edmondson recommends widening your lens to include **execution-as-learning**. Companies that use this approach focus not just on carrying out key processes more efficiently than rivals—but also on *learning* faster. To foster execution-as-learning, make it safe for employees to ask questions and fail. Then:

- Provide process guidelines, using the best available knowledge.

- Encourage collaborative decision-making.

- Collect process data describing how work unfolds.

- Use the data to identify process-improvement opportunities.

Through execution-as-learning, General Electric continually reinvents itself in multiple fields. Its 2007 profit? $22.5 billion.

The Idea in Practice. Edmondson provides these ideas for cultivating execution-as-learning in your firm:

Make It Safe. In psychologically safe environments, people offer ideas, questions, and concerns. They're willing to fail and when they do, they learn. To create a safe environment:

- Model openness, humility, and curiosity.

- Explicitly acknowledge the lack of answers to the tough problems facing your group.

- Ask questions showing that you genuinely want people's input.

- Reward learning.

Example: Pharmaceutical giant Eli Lilly's chief science officer introduced "failure parties" to honor intelligent experiments that failed.

Provide Process Guidelines. Even if you can't fully standardize knowledge work, you can provide process guidelines informed by best practices. Develop flexible guidelines, understanding that today's best practices won't be tomorrow's and won't work in every situation.

Example: Intermountain Healthcare assembled teams of experts on different diseases to develop detailed guidelines for treating patients with those conditions. Derived from analysis and debate among diverse professionals, the guidelines reflected the current best practices in the medical literature.

Encourage Collaborative Decision Making. Knowledge work requires people to make decisions together in response to unforeseen, novel, or complex problems. Provide tools enabling them to collaborate in real time.

Example: The Cleveland Clinic developed state-of-the-art IT systems that help dispersed caregivers who are participating in a patient's care to work together virtually. For instance, through an automated alert function, physicians learn of drugs others have prescribed. Medication decisions with interdependent consequences are thus made safely.

Collect Process Data. Gather data describing how work unfolds. Use it to determine what's going right and what's going wrong.

Example: Intermountain Healthcare allows doctors to deviate from the process guidelines anytime they judge that good patient care requires it. But doctors who deviate must help the organization learn by documenting what they did differently and why.

Identify Process-Improvement Opportunities. Analyze process data to improve the way activities are performed.

Example: At the Cleveland Clinic, seven teams of physicians focusing on specific conditions (heart failure, stroke, diabetes) study process data to identify areas for improvement throughout the organization's many sites. For instance, data showed that stroke patients treated at various sites had not always received a blood thinner within the three-hour window that research had identified as the standard of care. Analysis of patient outcomes helped make blood-thinner treatment the new standard of stroke care for all Cleveland Clinic hospitals. Consequently, hospitals doubled their use of blood thinner and reduced complications from stroke by 50%.

CHAPTER 6

The Hidden Benefits of Keeping Teams Intact

A few years ago one of us met an orthopedic surgeon with a reputation as the Henry Ford of knee replacements. Most surgeons take one to two hours to replace a knee, but this doctor routinely completes the procedure in 20 minutes. In a typical year he performs more than 550 knee replacements—2.5 times as many as the second-most-productive surgeon at his hospital and has better outcomes and fewer complications than many colleagues. During his 30-year career he has implemented dozens of techniques to improve his efficiency. For instance, he uses just one brand of prosthetic knee, and he opts for epidurals rather than general anesthesia. But another factor contributes to his speed: Although most surgeons work with an ever-changing cast of nurses and anesthesiologists, he has arranged to have two dedicated teams, one in each of two adjoining operating rooms; they include nurses who have worked alongside him for 18 years. He says that few of the methods he has pioneered would be practical if not for the easy familiarity of working with the same people every day.

Managers understand intuitively that team familiarity—the amount of experience individuals have working with one another—can influence how a group performs. But over the past seven years we've examined teams in corporate, health care, military, and consulting settings to understand team familiarity and quantify its benefits, and we've found that it is a much more profound phenomenon than most managers believe. They could and should be leveraging it to a far greater extent, especially in an era when teams are constantly forming, disbanding, and regrouping.

To do so they will need to overcome several barriers. Few organizations have integrated systems that track how frequently employees have worked together. Many managers put too much faith in shuffling rosters to prevent staleness and ensure fresh thinking. And realities such as cost pressures, developmental needs, travel limitations, and office politics often make familiarity hard to achieve. But organizations will benefit if leaders learn to surmount those barriers.

1.   Take Advantage of the Learning Curve

We aren't the first to investigate the importance of team familiarity. Prior research by academics such as the Harvard psychology professor Richard Hackman, who studied the performance of flight crews, has established that teams, like individuals, experience a learning curve. They generally do better as their members become familiar with one another. Other researchers have looked at how the performance of pro basketball teams varies according to how long players have been together. (See the sidebar "Stranger Danger.") In our work we have tried to better understand the degree to which performance improves with team familiarity, particularly in project-based environments in which so-called fluid teams frequently form and re-form.

Stranger Danger

Business isn't the only arena in which team familiarity improves performance. Research has shown that it's effective in other spheres as well.

The Hidden Benefits of Keeping Teams Intact

Defense

Leaders try to keep Special Ops teams, such as Navy Seals, intact. Over the past decade commanders of other units have also increased team familiarity, to better deal with dynamic environments such as Afghanistan.

Sports

A study of pro basketball teams found that familiarity reduced bad passes but teams with too much familiarity committed more errors, perhaps because their opponents could predict their moves.

Aviation

Research shows that 73% of commercial aviation incidents occur on a crew's first day of flying together. And a NASA study found that fatigued but familiar crews make about half as many errors as rested but unfamiliar ones.

Surgery

A study of surgeons who worked at multiple hospitals found that their performance varied from facility to facility—perhaps because of their varying levels of familiarity with the OR teams at different locations.

In a study conducted with the University of Oxford professor David Upton at the Bangalore-based software services firm Wipro, we examined 1,004 development projects involving 11,376 employees, using detailed personnel records to determine which employees had worked together before and to what extent. Then we looked at how well teams did, using criteria such as the number of defects in the software each team produced and the groups' adherence to deadlines and budgets. Rather than regard team familiarity as an all-or-nothing proposition, we constructed a continuous measure, counting the number of times team members had worked with one another over the previous three years and scaling the results according to the number of people on the team. We found that when familiarity increased by 50%, defects decreased by 19%, and deviations from budget decreased by 30%. We also found that familiarity was a better predictor of performance than the individual experience of team members or project managers.

At a software services firm, a **50%** increase in team familiarity was followed by a **19%** decrease in defects and a **30%** decrease in deviations from budget. On audit and consulting teams, high familiarity yielded a **10%** improvement in performance, as judged by clients.

In a second study at Wipro, we looked at how teams coped with the challenges of diverse experience among their members and found that although such diversity was generally associated with lower performance, teams with high degrees of familiarity were able to use it to improve. A third study one of us conducted with audit and consulting teams (in collaboration with Heidi Gardner and Francesca Gino, both of Harvard Business School) found a 10% improvement in performance, as judged by clients, when teams had members with a high degree of familiarity.

Why does team familiarity have such an outsize effect? Our research suggests that five factors are primarily responsible.

Coordinating activities.

Teams made up of diverse specialists are infamous for their inability to get things done. Despite the best-laid plans of the managers who assemble such teams, the differences among members frequently lead to poor communication, conflict, and confusion. Members new to one another simply don't understand when and how to communicate. Some groups never master this; and even in groups that do, the process takes time, slowing progress toward team goals. Familiarity can help a group overcome this obstacle: Once a team has learned when and how to communicate on one project, it can carry those skills over to the next.

Learning where knowledge lies.

Research shows that many teams struggle to tap the knowledge each individual brings to the task, because their members don't know who has what information. Unearthing this knowledge can take time and effort; the more frequently the same individuals work together, the better an organization amortizes this investment.

Responding to change.

Teams are increasingly asked to pivot mid-project because of competitive pressures or shifts in customer preferences. This creates stress and requires flexibility. Team familiarity provides a common platform from which the group can work to meet such new demands.

Integrating knowledge in order to innovate.

Innovative solutions typically come from new combinations of existing knowledge. For this to occur within a team, members must not only impart specific pieces of knowledge to one another but also integrate those isolated pieces of information. Because familiarity helps team members share information and communicate effectively, it makes them more likely to integrate knowledge and come up with a coherent, innovative solution.

Capturing value.

Organizations build competitive advantage when they create capabilities their competitors cannot replicate. Familiar teams are a key source of such advantage, because a competitor can't replicate an entire team's capabilities by hiring away an individual member. Each team member's performance is dependent on that of the others.

2. Create Better Teams

One of the benefits of using team familiarity as a tool is that implementation is relatively straightforward. The first step is to gain awareness. Managers should keep in mind the advantages of allowing individuals to work together frequently and make team assignments accordingly. If this sounds like a limiting factor, remember that a familiar team does not necessarily mean a dedicated team—one whose members rarely change, like the teams the superproductive knee surgeon had. A team with some degree of familiarity is better than a team with none. A little bit can go a long way.

We believe that many organizations should go beyond this first step and systematically measure and report on the prior experience individuals have working with one another. Organizations already use sophisticated IT systems to record employees' work histories and performance; in many cases, tracking familiarity would mean simply adding information to an existing system. Leading consulting firms, for instance, track what industries, customers, and types of projects each consultant has worked with. They should add familiarity—how many times specific combinations of workers have been on projects together—to the dimensions of experience they monitor.

The final step is to begin formally managing around the metric of team familiarity. This does not mean that the most-familiar team members should always be assigned to work together. It means realizing that because familiar teams perform better over the long term, it's in the organization's interest to cultivate familiarity. (For many managers, it also means learning to overcome the instinctive desire to shake things up.) That realization might lead a manager to place two less familiar workers on the same team—the experience they gain with each other will pay off in future projects. It might mean accepting the travel costs of including a far-flung employee. It might mean considering the benefits of team familiarity when deciding whether to try to retain a worker who's considering an outside job offer. It might also mean giving a key new executive wide latitude to hire former colleagues to join her on an important project.

Many questions about team familiarity remain. For instance, much of the existing research has focused on teams engaged in fairly routinized (albeit sophisticated) tasks, such as surgery, auditing, and piloting an aircraft. Team familiarity may not drive performance in more-innovative work—the kind done by the creative employees in an advertising agency or by the R&D group at a consumer products company. Indeed, although research has shown that familiarity can create the trust thought to be crucial for activities such as brainstorming, it may be that this benefit is trumped by the fresh perspectives that come from adding new voices to creative tasks. We also don't know much about how returns from team familiarity might change over time: Existing research suggests that in some contexts, people who work together *too* long become stale and see their performance drop.

What we do know is that in many cases, people who have collaborated before will work better together than people who haven't—and that most organizations could do a far better job of exploiting this simple but powerful insight.

***

Balancing "We" and "Me"

CHAPTER 7
Balancing "We" and "Me"

The open office is the dominant form of workspace design for good reason: It fosters collaboration, promotes learning, and nurtures strong culture. But what most companies fail to realize is that collaboration has a natural rhythm that requires both interaction and private contemplation.

Companies have been trying for decades to find the balance between public and private workspace that best supports collaboration. In 1980 52% of U.S. employees lacked workspaces where they could concentrate without distraction. In response, high-walled cubicles took over the corporate landscape. By the late 1990s, the tide had turned, and only 23% of employees wanted more privacy, and 50% wanted more access to other people. Ever since, firms have been beefing up spaces that support collaboration and shrinking areas for individual work. But the pendulum seems to have swung too far: Once again, people feel a pressing need for privacy, not only to do heads-down work but to cope with the intensity of work today.

To address these needs, according to the authors, we have to rethink our assumptions about privacy. Traditionally defined in physical terms, privacy is now about the individual's ability to control *information* and *stimulation*. In this article, the authors examine workspace design through the new lens of privacy and offer insights on how to foster teamwork and solitude.

The open office has a lot of critics these days. But it remains the dominant form of workplace design for a reason: It can foster collaboration, promote learning, and nurture a strong culture. It's the right idea; unfortunately, it's often poorly executed—even as a way to support collaboration.

There's a natural rhythm to collaboration. People need to focus alone or in pairs to generate ideas or process information; then they come together as a group to build on those ideas or develop a shared point of view; and then they break apart again to take next steps. The more demanding the collaboration task is, the more individuals need punctuating moments of private time to think or recharge.

Companies have been trying for decades to find the balance between public and private workspace that best supports collaboration. In 1980 our research found that 85% of U.S. employees said they needed places to concentrate without distractions, and 52% said they lacked such spaces. In response, thousands of high-walled cubicles took over the corporate landscape. By the late 1990s, the tide had turned, and only 23% of employees wanted more privacy; 50% said they needed more access to other people, and 40% wanted more interaction. Organizations responded by shifting their real estate allocation toward open spaces that support collaboration and shrinking areas for individual work. But the pendulum may have swung too far: Our research now suggests that once again, people feel a pressing need for more privacy, not only to do heads-down work but to cope with the intensity of how work happens today.

Inside the U.S. Workplace

Today more than 70% of employees work in an open office environment, and the size of their individual workspaces is shrinking.

The open plan is just one of the culprits assaulting our privacy. The increased focus on collaborative work means we're rarely alone, and the ubiquity of mobile devices means we're always accessible. In light of these pressures, it's not surprising that the number of people who say they can't concentrate at their desk has increased by 16% since 2008, and the number of those who don't have access to quiet places to do focused work is up by 13%. Meanwhile, people are finding it harder to control who has access to their personal information, at work and elsewhere. In fact, 74% of the people we surveyed said they're more concerned about their privacy now than they were 10 years ago.

Leaving the office to work at home or in coffee shops or libraries isn't the answer—at least not for the long term. Too much remote work creates its own set of problems, such as diminished knowledge transfer, decreased engagement, cultural disconnect, and a slew of new distractions. And, of course, it makes collaboration more difficult.

Steelcase has been exploring the issue of privacy since the 1980s, and over the years we've worked with thousands of organizations in many industries to develop open office environments. Recently we conducted a study of workplaces and workers in Europe, North America, and Asia, using surveys, ethnographic research, observations, and interviews to update our understanding. Here we present new insights into the nature of privacy and offer strategies that allow employees to get away without going away.

The Big Differences Between Satisfied and Dissatisfied Workers

Results from a 2014 survey on well-being in the office.

Manage Distraction

% of respondents who agree that their work environment allows them to concentrate easily

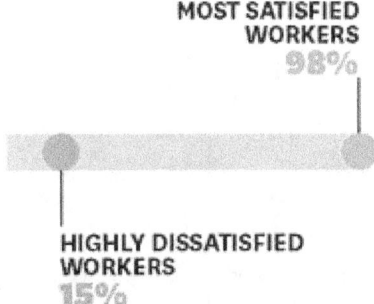

**MOST SATISFIED
WORKERS**
98%

**HIGHLY DISSATISFIED
WORKERS**
15%

Take a Break

% of respondents who agree that they can socialize and have informal, relaxed conversations with their colleagues

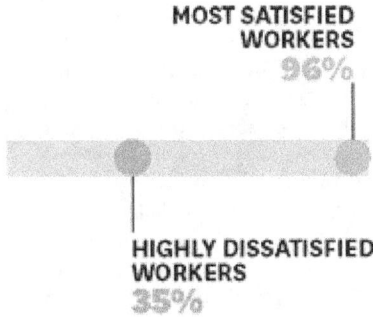

**MOST SATISFIED
WORKERS**
96%

**HIGHLY DISSATISFIED
WORKERS**
35%

Work Where You Want

% of respondents who agree that they can choose where they wish to work within the office according to the task at hand

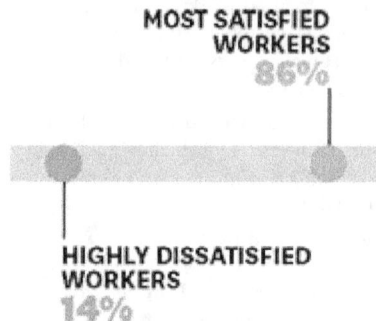

MOST SATISFIED WORKERS 86%

HIGHLY DISSATISFIED WORKERS 14%

Avoid Interruptions

% of respondents who agree that they can work in teams without being disrupted

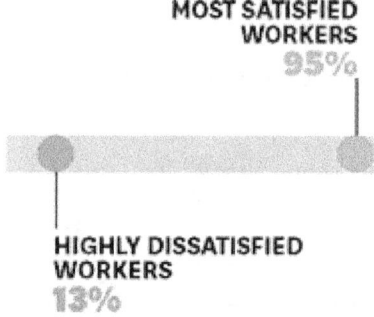

MOST SATISFIED WORKERS 95%

HIGHLY DISSATISFIED WORKERS 13%

Redefining Privacy at Work

Researchers and architects have traditionally defined privacy at work in physical terms: acoustical (Can we hear each other?), visual (Can we see each other?), and territorial (Do I have a place that's just for me?). But in today's workplace, we're always connected, always reachable, and to some extent always findable, in both the physical and the virtual sense. That accessibility can enhance our interactions but can also leave us feeling overexposed.

So we need to rethink our basic assumptions about privacy. At Steelcase, we believe that privacy has two distinct dimensions.

Information control.

Employees today wage a constant battle to protect and manage access to their personal information. Over the course of a day, we shift constantly between revealing and concealing aspects of ourselves and our work to and from others: Who needs access to these project files? How can I keep coworkers from seeing sensitive information on my computer screen? Where can I have a confidential conversation without being overheard? Can I read an article or check my Twitter feed at my desk without fear that people will think I'm slacking?

Technology has further challenged our sense of personal sovereignty. Social media in particular have done more than any other force to compromise our ability to control our information. Facebook, for example, allows us to curate what we share about ourselves—but only up to a point. Even those who opt out of popular social media sites have a hard time hiding from Google. What if we really don't want coworkers to know where we live, what religion we practice, what music we listen to, or how old we are? We have to make conscious decisions about how we manage our personal information and act on those decisions vigilantly. If we don't—and most of us don't—then we're left feeling uncomfortably vulnerable.

Stimulation control.

The second dimension of privacy encompasses the noises and other distractions that break concentration or inhibit the ability to focus. Stimulation control is in some ways more variable and idiosyncratic than information control. One person's distraction may be another's comforting white noise. And on any given day, our notion of distraction can change. Sometimes we might find background music soothing; other times it might be annoying. However we define them, we all need ways to manage distractions.

Fundamentally, stimulation control governs the ability to focus attention. In thinking about office design, it's helpful to understand that neuroscience research identifies three basic modes of attention. The first is *controlled attention:* working on a task that requires intense focus, such as writing or thinking deeply, while willfully avoiding unrelated thoughts and inhibiting external stimuli. When we are in this mode, interruptions and other distractions are unwelcome, and our need to control the environment around us increases.

The second mode is *stimulus-driven attention:* switching focus when something catches our attention. When we're performing routine tasks—responding to e-mails, scheduling meetings, or catching up on other administrative work—we may tolerate or even welcome interruptions or distractions. Many people choose to perform routine tasks in open, social, or active settings.

We call the third mode *rejuvenation*—the periodic respites from concentration that we take throughout the day. It's a time-out for our brains and bodies and often a chance to engage socially with others or express emotions that we've kept on a tight leash. For rejuvenation, people may seek either a highly stimulating environment or a quiet one, depending on personal preference.

The need to control stimulation as we switch among the three modes means that we require a variety of workspaces that afford more or less privacy. The challenge is to find the right balance of social and private and to provide spaces that enhance all three modes.

Redefining Privacy

The ubiquity of electronic devices and connectivity means that privacy in the workplace can no longer be thought of strictly in physical terms. Today privacy is about employees' need to control *information* and *stimulation* in three key realms.

Privacy Across Cultures

While the need for privacy is universal, the ways it is experienced across cultures vary. To better understand the similarities and differences around the world, Steelcase partnered with the global research firm Ipsos to conduct surveys in 14 countries; we then synthesized the data with our ongoing ethnographic research. Most findings were consistent with earlier research, but a few surprised us.

Attitudes toward personal space differ greatly from country to country. Germans allocate an average of 320 square feet per employee; Americans, an average of 190. For workers in India and China, the figures are 70 and 50 square feet respectively. Yet despite their relatively dense workspaces, both Indian and Chinese workers rated their work environments highly in terms of their ability to concentrate and work without disruption.

That finding points to a significant cultural difference. In China people don't think about individual privacy in the same way that Westerners do. Chinese workers are most concerned about information control: keeping personal data private and seeking refuge from the feeling of being watched. Thus, in China, where offices are organized so that managers can easily keep tabs on workers, people tend to duck into hallways or bathrooms for a moment alone. Offices that allow workers to have their backs to the wall are considered prime real estate. In

India it's not uncommon for workers to seek out pockets of privacy—in unoccupied nooks on the periphery of workspaces, in storage areas, or along walls.

	Outgoing INFORMATION	Incoming STIMULATION
SOCIAL	How much do I want colleagues to know about my personal interests? Should I connect with colleagues on social media?	How can I limit interruptions by coworkers? How can I avoid constant exposure to the noise and activity of others?
TECHNOLOGICAL	Can I opt out of giving biometric data used for security purposes? Can I shield my name from feedback to superiors?	Do I want pop-up previews of incoming e-mails? I need to focus: Is it OK to turn off instant messaging?
SPATIAL	Can people see my computer screen while I'm working? What personal photos or artifacts do I want to display?	What space configuration minimizes my exposure to flickering fluorescent lights? How can I block out my neighbor's phone conversations?

Among Western workers, by contrast, the issue of stimulation control tends to take center stage: Only 55% of the workers we surveyed said they are able to work in groups without being interrupted. Less than half say they can choose where they want to work within the office on the basis of the task at hand. In our research, the adjective Americans used most frequently to describe their workplaces was "stressful." The adjective Chinese workers used most was "calming." (Then again, it's perfectly acceptable in China to take a nap at work.)

When it comes to heads-down focus, however, American workers give their office environments relatively high marks, despite the vocal complaints heard in social media and other forums. A surprising 70% of workers in the United States say their workplace provides the ability to concentrate easily. Because cubicles still dominate the North American office landscape, and more real estate is allocated for individual workspaces than for collaboration activities, we believe that the reported frustrations are quite likely being exacerbated by factors other than the physical environment such as the intense pace of work.

Overall, workers in European countries (except in the Netherlands) were the most dissatisfied with their ability to control their privacy and were more likely to be dissatisfied with their work environment in general. Of the workers in our survey who ranked as the most highly dissatisfied and disengaged, 53% came from France, Germany, Spain, and Belgium. The cultural norm in those countries is that work happens in the office, generally at an assigned workspace, and opportunities to seek solitude or achieve greater levels of privacy are often limited. In the Netherlands, by contrast, there's greater comfort with letting people work from a diverse range of spaces, inside and outside the office. Moreover, the Dutch are more egalitarian than their neighbors when it comes to office design. Privacy considerations are not based on status, and leaders work alongside employees of all levels in open spaces. This might explain why the Dutch accounted for almost half of satisfied and engaged employees. (For a country-by-country comparison, see the exhibit "How Employees Feel About the Workplace.")

How Employees Feel About the Workplace

We surveyed employees around the world on three dimensions of privacy critical to workplace satisfaction. Surprisingly, Indian and Chinese workers, who have significantly smaller individual spaces and denser office environments, ranked highest.

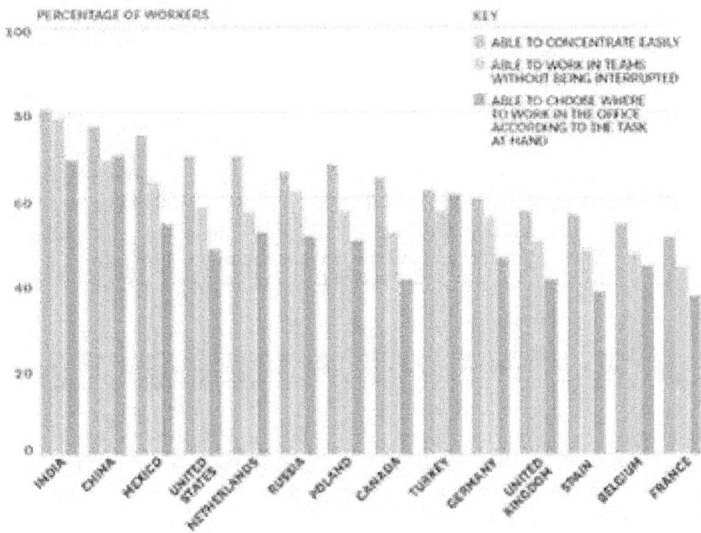

While privacy means different things in different cultures, our study showed that workplace satisfaction and engagement are deeply connected to a sense of control over one's environment. In our study, 98% of the most highly engaged employees reported that they had "the ability to concentrate easily" in their workplace and that this attribute is a top factor in their satisfaction. They also scored high on "being able to work in teams without being disrupted" and "being able to choose where to work according to the task at hand"—other factors critical to high engagement and satisfaction. Conversely, highly disengaged and dissatisfied employees struggled with disruptions and felt they had very little control over where or how they worked. Only 15% said they could concentrate easily.

Personal Strategies for Privacy

In addition to local culture, factors such as organizational culture, the type of task one is engaged in, mood, and individual personality shape how much privacy people require and the way they achieve it. For example, introverts tend to gravitate toward places where they feel that they have the most control over stimulation. Susan Cain's recent study of introverts argues that they are not shy; rather, they are more sensitive to stimuli than extroverts are. Our research pointed to five privacy strategies that people use, sometimes unconsciously, to control both stimulation and information.

Strategic anonymity.

Some of us find deep privacy in the middle of a crowd of strangers. When people go to a café to do focused work, they are often trying to inhibit the social distractions they face in their workplace. Recent research by Ravi Mehta, Rui Zhu, and Amar Cheema in the *Journal of Consumer Research* shows that working in an environment with a moderate level of ambient background noise can enhance performance on creative tasks. Many people enjoy the hum of activity in cafés or airports, where they can work, read, or relax without disruption. The key is that it's strategic: Individuals choose when and how to make themselves anonymous.

Selective exposure.

In today's world, where our personal information is being shared and demanded across new channels in exponentially higher degrees, the boundaries between what is and isn't private are constantly shifting. People choose to reveal some information to certain people or groups, while sharing different information with others. In the physical sense, this may mean choosing whether to share a particular document with a coworker or deciding what personal artifacts to display at work. It could also be about making a decision to use the phone instead of video chat if we don't want others to be able to see us.

Entrusted confidence.

Privacy doesn't just mean being alone. There are many contexts in the workplace where groups of individuals need to have private conversations. Some moments of entrusted confidence, such as performance reviews, may be scheduled and planned. More often, they happen spontaneously, such as when colleagues need to discuss a sensitive problem that has cropped up; and at these times it can be difficult to find an available conference room. In workplaces that are highly open, we see greater demand for dedicated conference or project rooms that teams or individuals can easily access, where they feel secure sharing confidences.

Intentional shielding.

People talk about feeling "violated" when they think they're being watched or eavesdropped on. They use a variety of shielding tactics to protect themselves. We often see people go to an enclosed location to take a call, or walk in public areas where they are less likely to be overheard. Many people avoid working in spaces where they can't see coworkers approaching. Others engage in intentional shielding by keeping their own counsel, protecting their individual thoughts and ideas so that they can develop a point of view without the distracting influence of "groupthink" or peer pressure.

Purposeful solitude.

Isolation is largely a matter of circumstance and state of mind: Your physical location, your habits, and your attitudes can all conspire to make you feel isolated from a group. But solitude is intentional; you make a conscious choice to separate from a group in order to concentrate, recharge, express emotion, or engage in personal activities. Some people may choose a closed space where they have visual and acoustical privacy if they need respite or to focus intently on a project. Others may choose to eat lunch in the farthest empty corner of a cafeteria. Stepping outside to sit in a quiet courtyard and taking a short walk are other ways people seek alone time.

Organizational Strategies for Privacy

As organizations come to understand the need for privacy at work, they must also recognize that privacy does not compromise collaboration. By improving privacy you can actually enrich and strengthen collaborative activities.

Organizations have a range of strategies they can implement, but the success of any of them depends on a supporting culture that gives employees control over where and how they work and how they manage their privacy. Cultures are built and reinforced when people exhibit certain behaviors over time and those behaviors are articulated, adopted, and embraced across the organization. Leaders who model the desired behaviors give implicit permission to others to follow suit and send the message "This is how we work here."

Employees can use a host of props or devices to establish boundaries, but gadgets won't work unless they're backed up by a culture that respects the need for privacy.

Some strategies demand an investment in new kinds of space, but others require only modest reconfigurations along with behavioral and cultural changes. Here are four effective options:

Protocols.

Organizations can lay down rules that define acceptable behaviors about privacy. Protocols can be companywide or specific to certain departments, times, or places. For example, an organization might choose to designate a particular time for quiet work in one or multiple locations. Or it might decide that music or videos should be a headphones-only experience. Leaders should communicate the protocols clearly and explain the rationales behind them. Many workplace protocols have gone by the wayside when people don't understand them or forget what type of behavior is appropriate. To sustain the adoption of these practices, encourage supportive but honest conversations when protocols are broken and clearly communicate the consequences for repeat offenses.

Signaling.

Signals are similar to protocols, but rather than being established by the organization, they are adopted by employees themselves to communicate their privacy requirements to others. In many offices earbuds are an accepted way of signaling "do not disturb"; some people wear noise-canceling headphones to make their point even more obvious. People can also signal a desire for privacy by how they orient themselves in a room: Facing others encourages interaction; tucking behind a screen or a large plant says "I'm trying to be alone."

Employees can find a host of props or devices to help them establish privacy boundaries with their coworkers. But even the most sophisticated gadget won't work unless it's backed up by a culture that respects the individual's need for privacy. Leaders should make it clear that employees must respect privacy signals in open spaces and support individuals' efforts to control their information and stimulation.

Strategic space planning.

There are two primary design approaches for accommodating privacy needs in the physical workspace: the distributed model and the zone model. In the distributed model, spaces that support stimulation control are blended into areas for both individual and group work. This model makes it easy for people to shift quickly between modes of work. For instance, a worker may need to focus deeply while preparing for a meeting, move to a nearby project room to collaborate, and afterward break away with one other person to concentrate on a task. Physical proximity of these spaces facilitates quick switching between work modes.

The zone model defines certain locations within the larger workplace as private, quiet spaces. Organizations may designate a particular area or even an entire floor or building as a sort of "library" or quiet hub. In this model, the private zones are physically separate from open areas. This approach can be especially useful in managing noise disruptions.

An ecosystem of spaces.

Our studies show that the most successful work environments provide a range of spaces— an ecosystem—that allow people to choose where and how they get their jobs done.

In some situations, individuals need their own enclosed space for regular use. But design and allocation of such space needs to shift from being hierarchy-based to being needs-based. For example, many executives are granted spacious, enclosed offices that often sit empty because of travel or meeting schedules. These could be redesigned to allow other people to use them productively when their primary users are off-site. Like others in the organization, many leaders simply need access to an enclosed space for certain tasks when they are on-site.

Whether owned or shared, enclosed spaces are more effective when they allow users to control stimulation. Sound, for instance, travels like water, seeping through partitions and gaps in walls and ceilings. Enclosed spaces make it easier to avoid overhearing conversations that everyone prefers to keep private. Such spaces should also take into account visual distractions. The trend toward greater transparency has led to more glass walls, especially in spaces that are situated near windows, but they can lead to the unpleasant feeling of "working in a fishbowl." A simple band of frosted glass does a great deal to reinforce the privacy of such areas.

"Shielded" spaces can also be used to provide sufficient privacy for many tasks. These areas are generally semi-enclosed, made with partial-height walls or portable screens. When combined with appropriate protocols, the boundaries signal "Do not disturb." They are particularly effective when placed in quiet zones. They're also a low-cost solution: In one of our spaces, designers used everyday objects such as books and plants and simple configurations of the furnishings to discourage conversations. Without any explicit communication, the space clearly told people that it was intended for individual, quiet work. Open offices are not inherently good or bad. The key to successful workspaces is to empower individuals by giving them choices that allow control over their work environment. When they can choose where and how they work, they have more capacity to draw energy and ideas from others and be re-energized by moments of solitude. Providing the ability to move easily between group time and individual private time creates a rhythm—coming together to think about a problem and then going away to let ideas gestate—that is essential to the modern organization.

CHAPTER 8
Managing Multicultural Teams

Multicultural teams offer a number of advantages to international firms, including deep knowledge of different product markets, culturally sensitive customer service, and 24-hour work rotations. But those advantages may be outweighed by problems stemming from cultural differences, which can seriously impair the effectiveness of a team or even bring it to a stalemate. How can managers best cope with culture-based challenges?

The authors conducted in-depth interviews with managers and members of multicultural teams from all over the world. Drawing on their extensive research on dispute resolution and teamwork and those interviews, they identify four problem categories that can create barriers to a team's success: direct versus indirect communication, trouble with accents and fluency, differing attitudes toward hierarchy and authority, and conflicting norms for decision making. If a manager—or a team member—can pinpoint the root cause of the problem, he or she is likelier to select an appropriate strategy for solving it.

The most successful teams and managers, the authors found, dealt with multicultural challenges in one of four ways: adaptation (acknowledging cultural gaps openly and working around them), structural intervention (changing the shape or makeup of the team), managerial intervention (setting norms early or bringing in a higher-level manager), and exit (removing a team member when other options have failed). Which strategy is best depends on the particular circumstances—and each has potential complications. In general, though, managers who intervene early and set norms; teams and managers who try to engage everyone on the team; and teams that can see challenges as stemming from culture, not personality, succeed in solving culture-based problems with good humor and creativity. They are the likeliest to harvest the benefits inherent in multicultural teams.

When a major international software developer needed to produce a new product quickly, the project manager assembled a team of employees from India and the United States. From the start the team members could not agree on a delivery date for the product. The Americans thought the work could be done in two to three weeks; the Indians predicted it would take two to three months. As time went on, the Indian team members proved reluctant to report setbacks in the production process, which the American team members would find out about only when work was due to be passed to them. Such conflicts, of course, may affect any team, but in this case they arose from cultural differences. As tensions mounted, conflict over delivery dates and feedback became personal, disrupting team members' communication about even mundane issues. The project manager decided he had to intervene with the result that both the American and the Indian team members came to rely on him for direction regarding minute operational details that the team should have been able to handle itself. The manager became so bogged down by quotidian issues that the project careened hopelessly off even the most pessimistic schedule and the team never learned to work together effectively.

Multicultural teams often generate frustrating management dilemmas. Cultural differences can create substantial obstacles to effective teamwork but these may be subtle and difficult to recognize until significant damage has already been done. As in the case above, which the manager involved told us about, managers may create more problems than they resolve by intervening. The challenge in managing multicultural teams effectively is to recognize underlying cultural causes of conflict, and to intervene in ways that both get the team back on track and empower its members to deal with future challenges themselves.

We interviewed managers and members of multicultural teams from all over the world. These interviews, combined with our deep research on dispute resolution and teamwork, led us to conclude that the wrong kind of managerial intervention may sideline valuable members who should be participating or, worse, create resistance, resulting in poor team performance. We're not talking here about respecting differing national standards for doing business, such as accounting practices. We're referring to day-to-day working problems among team members that can keep multicultural teams from realizing the very gains they were set up to harvest, such as knowledge of different product markets, culturally sensitive customer service, and 24-hour work rotations.

The good news is that cultural challenges are manageable if managers and team members choose the right strategy and avoid imposing single-culture-based approaches on multicultural situations.

The Challenges. People tend to assume that challenges on multicultural teams arise from differing styles of communication. But this is only one of the four categories that, according to our research, can create barriers to a team's ultimate success. These categories are direct versus indirect communication; trouble with accents and fluency; differing attitudes toward hierarchy and authority; and conflicting norms for decision making.

Direct versus indirect communication. Communication in Western cultures is typically direct and explicit. The meaning is on the surface, and a listener doesn't have to know much about the context or the speaker to interpret it. This is not true in many other cultures, where meaning is embedded in the way the message is presented. For example, Western negotiators get crucial information about the other party's preferences and priorities by asking direct questions, such as "Do you prefer option A or option B?" In cultures that use indirect communication, negotiators may have to infer preferences and priorities from changes or the lack of them in the other party's settlement proposal. In cross-cultural negotiations, the non-Westerner can understand the direct communications of the Westerner, but the Westerner has difficulty understanding the indirect communications of the non-Westerner.

Communication in Western cultures is typically direct and explicit. In many other cultures, meaning is embedded in the way the message is presented. The differences can cause serious damage to team relationships.

An American manager who was leading a project to build an interface for a U.S. and Japanese customer-data system explained the problems her team was having this way: "In Japan, they want to talk and discuss. Then we take a break and they talk within the organization. They want to make sure that there's harmony in the rest of the organization. One of the hardest lessons for me was when I thought they were saying yes but they just meant 'I'm listening to you.'"

The differences between direct and indirect communication can cause serious damage to relationships when team projects run into problems. When the American manager quoted above discovered that several flaws in the system would significantly disrupt company operations, she pointed this out in an e-mail to her American boss and the Japanese team members. Her boss appreciated the direct warnings; her Japanese colleagues were embarrassed, because she had violated their norms for uncovering and discussing problems. Their reaction was to provide her with less access to the people and information she needed to monitor progress. They would probably have responded better if she had pointed out the problems indirectly—for example, by asking them what would happen if a certain part of the system was not functioning properly, even though she knew full well that it was malfunctioning and also what the implications were.

As our research indicates is so often true, communication challenges create barriers to effective teamwork by reducing information sharing, creating interpersonal conflict, or both. In Japan, a typical response to direct confrontation is to isolate the norm violator. This

American manager was isolated not just socially but also physically. She told us, "They literally put my office in a storage room, where I had desks stacked from floor to ceiling and I was the only person there. So they totally isolated me, which was a pretty loud signal to me that I was not a part of the inside circle and that they would communicate with me only as needed."

Her direct approach had been intended to solve a problem, and in one sense, it did, because her project was launched problem-free. But her norm violations exacerbated the challenges of working with her Japanese colleagues and limited her ability to uncover any other problems that might have derailed the project later on.

Trouble with accents and fluency. Although the language of international business is English, misunderstandings or deep frustration may occur because of nonnative speakers' accents, lack of fluency, or problems with translation or usage. These may also influence perceptions of status or competence.

For example, a Latin American member of a multicultural consulting team lamented, "Many times I felt that because of the language difference, I didn't have the words to say some things that I was thinking. I noticed that when I went to these interviews with the U.S. guy, he would tend to lead the interviews, which was understandable but also disappointing, because we are at the same level. I had very good questions, but he would take the lead."

When we interviewed an American member of a U.S.-Japanese team that was assessing the potential expansion of a U.S. retail chain into Japan, she described one American teammate this way: "He was not interested in the Japanese consultants' feedback and felt that because they weren't as fluent as he was, they weren't intelligent enough and, therefore, could add no value." The team member described was responsible for assessing one aspect of the feasibility of expansion into Japan. Without input from the Japanese experts, he risked overestimating opportunities and underestimating challenges.

Nonfluent team members may well be the most expert on the team, but their difficulty communicating knowledge makes it hard for the team to recognize and utilize their expertise. If teammates become frustrated or impatient with a lack of fluency, interpersonal conflicts can arise. Nonnative speakers may become less motivated to contribute, or anxious about their performance evaluations and future career prospects. The organization as a whole pays a greater price: Its investment in a multicultural team fails to pay off.

Some teams, we learned, use language differences to resolve (rather than create) tensions. A team of U.S. and Latin American buyers was negotiating with a team from a Korean supplier. The negotiations took place in Korea, but the discussions were conducted in English. Frequently the Koreans would caucus at the table by speaking Korean. The buyers, frustrated, would respond by appearing to caucus in Spanish though they discussed only inconsequential current events and sports, in case any of the Koreans spoke Spanish. Members of the team who didn't speak Spanish pretended to participate, to the great amusement of their teammates. This approach proved effective: It conveyed to the Koreans in an appropriately indirect way that their caucuses in Korean were frustrating and annoying to the other side. As a result, both teams cut back on sidebar conversations.

Differing attitudes toward hierarchy and authority. A challenge inherent in multicultural teamwork is that by design, teams have a rather flat structure. But team members from some cultures, in which people are treated differently according to their status in an organization, are uncomfortable on flat teams. If they defer to higher-status team members, their behavior will be seen as appropriate when most of the team comes from a hierarchical culture; but they may damage their stature and credibility—and even face humiliation—if most of the team comes from an egalitarian culture.

Team members who are uncomfortable on flat teams may, by deferring to higher-status teammates, damage their stature and credibility and even face humiliation if most of the team is from an egalitarian culture.

One manager of Mexican heritage, who was working on a credit and underwriting team for a bank, told us, "In Mexican culture, you're always supposed to be humble. So whether you understand something or not, you're supposed to put it in the form of a question. You have to keep it open-ended, out of respect. I think that actually worked against me, because the Americans thought I really didn't know what I was talking about. So it made me feel like they thought I was wavering on my answer."

When, as a result of differing cultural norms, team members believe they've been treated disrespectfully, the whole project can blow up. In another Korean-U.S. negotiation, the American members of a due diligence team were having difficulty getting information from their Korean counterparts, so they complained directly to higher-level Korean management, nearly wrecking the deal. The higher-level managers were offended because hierarchy is strictly adhered to in Korean organizations and culture. It should have been their own lower-level people, not the U.S. team members, who came to them with a problem. And the Korean team members were mortified that their bosses had been involved before they themselves could brief them. The crisis was resolved only when high-level U.S. managers made a trip to Korea, conveying appropriate respect for their Korean counterparts.

Conflicting norms for decision making. Cultures differ enormously when it comes to decision making particularly, how quickly decisions should be made and how much analysis is required beforehand. Not surprisingly, U.S. managers like to make decisions very quickly and with relatively little analysis by comparison with managers from other countries.

A Brazilian manager at an American company who was negotiating to buy Korean products destined for Latin America told us, "On the first day, we agreed on three points, and on the second day, the U.S.-Spanish side wanted to start with point four. But the Korean side wanted to go back and rediscuss points one through three. My boss almost had an attack."

What U.S. team members learn from an experience like this is that the American way simply cannot be imposed on other cultures. Managers from other cultures may, for example, decline to share information until they understand the full scope of a project. But they have learned that they can't simply ignore the desire of their American counterparts to make decisions quickly. What to do? The best solution seems to be to make minor concessions on process to learn to adjust to and even respect another approach to decision making. For example, American managers have learned to keep their impatient bosses away from team meetings and give them frequent if brief updates. A comparable lesson for managers from other cultures is to be explicit about what they need—saying, for example, "We have to see the big picture before we talk details."

Four Strategies. The most successful teams and managers we interviewed used four strategies for dealing with these challenges: adaptation (acknowledging cultural gaps openly and working around them), structural intervention (changing the shape of the team), managerial intervention (setting norms early or bringing in a higher-level manager), and exit (removing a team member when other options have failed). There is no one right way to deal with a particular kind of multicultural problem; identifying the type of challenge is only the first step. The more crucial step is assessing the circumstances—or "enabling situational conditions"—under which the team is working. For example, does the project allow any flexibility for change, or do deadlines make that impossible? Are there additional resources available that might be tapped? Is the team permanent or temporary? Does the team's manager have the autonomy to make a decision about changing the team in some way? Once the situational conditions have been analyzed, the team's leader can identify an appropriate response (see the exhibit "Identifying the Right Strategy").

Identifying the Right Strategy. The most successful teams and managers we interviewed use four strategies for dealing with problems: adaptation (acknowledging cultural gaps openly and working around them), structural intervention (changing the shape of the team), managerial intervention (setting norms early or bringing in a higher-level manager), and exit (removing a team member when other options have failed). Adaptation is the ideal strategy because the team works effectively to solve its own problem with minimal input from management—and, most important, learns from the experience. The guide below can help you identify the right strategy once you have identified both the problem and the "enabling situational conditions" that apply to the team.

REPRESENTATIVE PROBLEMS	ENABLING SITUATIONAL CONDITIONS	STRATEGY	COMPLICATING FACTORS
• Conflict arises from decision-making differences • Misunderstanding or stonewalling arises from communication differences	• Team members can attribute a challenge to culture rather than personality • Higher-level managers are not available or the team would be embarrassed to involve them	Adaptation	• Team members must be exceptionally aware • Negotiating a common understanding takes time
• The team is affected by emotional tensions relating to fluency issues or prejudice • Team members are inhibited by perceived status differences among teammates	• The team can be subdivided to mix cultures or expertise • Tasks can be subdivided	Structural Intervention	• If team members aren't carefully distributed, subgroups can strengthen preexisting differences • Subgroup solutions have to fit back together
• Violations of hierarchy have resulted in loss of face • An absence of ground rules is causing conflict	• The problem has produced a high level of emotion • The team has reached a stalemate • A higher-level manager is able and willing to intervene	Managerial Intervention	• The team becomes overly dependent on the manager • Team members may be sidelined or resistant
• A team member cannot adjust to the challenge at hand and has become unable to contribute to the project	• The team is permanent rather than temporary • Emotions are beyond the point of intervention • Too much face has been lost	Exit	• Talent and training costs are lost

Adaptation. Some teams find ways to work with or around the challenges they face, adapting practices or attitudes without making changes to the group's membership or assignments. Adaptation works when team members are willing to acknowledge and name their cultural differences and to assume responsibility for figuring out how to live with them. It's often the best possible approach to a problem, because it typically involves less managerial time than other strategies; and because team members participate in solving the problem themselves, they learn from the process. When team members have this mind-set, they can be creative about protecting their own substantive differences while acceding to the processes of others.

An American software engineer located in Ireland who was working with an Israeli account management team from his own company told us how shocked he was by the Israelis' in-your-face style: "There were definitely different ways of approaching issues and discussing them. There is something pretty common to the Israeli culture: They like to argue. I tend to try to collaborate more, and it got very stressful for me until I figured out how to kind of merge the cultures."

The software engineer adapted. He imposed some structure on the Israelis that helped him maintain his own style of being thoroughly prepared; that accommodation enabled him to accept the Israeli style. He also noticed that team members weren't just confronting him; they confronted one another but were able to work together effectively nevertheless. He realized that the confrontation was not personal but cultural.

In another example, an American member of a postmerger consulting team was frustrated by the hierarchy of the French company his team was working with. He felt that a meeting with certain French managers who were not directly involved in the merger "wouldn't deliver any value to me or for purposes of the project," but said that he had come to understand that "it was very important to really involve all the people there" if the integration was ultimately to work.

A U.S. and UK multicultural team tried to use their differing approaches to decision making to reach a higher-quality decision. This approach, called fusion, is getting serious attention from political scientists and from government officials dealing with multicultural populations that want to protect their cultures rather than integrate or assimilate. If the team had relied exclusively on the Americans' "forge ahead" approach, it might not have recognized the pitfalls that lay ahead and might later have had to back up and start over. Meanwhile, the UK members would have been gritting their teeth and saying "We told you things were moving too fast." If the team had used the "Let's think about this" UK approach, it might have wasted a lot of time trying to identify every pitfall, including the most unlikely, while the U.S. members chomped at the bit and muttered about analysis paralysis. The strength of this team was that some of its members were willing to forge ahead and some were willing to work through pitfalls. To accommodate them all, the team did both—moving not quite as fast as the U.S. members would have on their own and not quite as thoroughly as the UK members would have.

Structural intervention. A structural intervention is a deliberate reorganization or reassignment designed to reduce interpersonal friction or to remove a source of conflict for one or more groups. This approach can be extremely effective when obvious subgroups demarcate the team (for example, headquarters versus national subsidiaries) or if team members are proud, defensive, threatened, or clinging to negative stereotypes of one another.

A member of an investment research team scattered across continental Europe, the UK, and the U.S. described for us how his manager resolved conflicts stemming from status differences and language tensions among the team's three "tribes." The manager started by having the team meet face-to-face twice a year, not to discuss mundane day-to-day problems (of which there were many) but to identify a set of values that the team would use to direct and evaluate its progress. At the first meeting, he realized that when he started to speak, everyone else "shut down," waiting to hear what he had to say. So he hired a consultant to run future meetings. The consultant didn't represent a hierarchical threat and was therefore able to get lots of participation from team members.

Another structural intervention might be to create smaller working groups of mixed cultures or mixed corporate identities in order to get at information that is not forthcoming from the team as a whole. The manager of the team that was evaluating retail opportunities in Japan used this approach. When she realized that the female Japanese consultants would not participate if the group got large, or if their male superior was present, she broke the team up into smaller groups to try to solve problems. She used this technique repeatedly and made a point of changing the subgroups' membership each time so that team members got to know and respect everyone else on the team.

The subgrouping technique involves risks, however. It buffers people who are not working well together or not participating in the larger group for one reason or another. Sooner or later the team will have to assemble the pieces that the subgroups have come up with, so this approach relies on another structural intervention: Someone must become a mediator in order to see that the various pieces fit together.

Managerial intervention. When a manager behaves like an arbitrator or a judge, making a final decision without team involvement, neither the manager nor the team gains much insight into why the team has stalemated. But it is possible for team members to use managerial intervention effectively to sort out problems.

When an American refinery-safety expert with significant experience throughout East Asia got stymied during a project in China, she called in her company's higher-level managers in Beijing to talk to the higher-level managers to whom the Chinese refinery's managers reported. Unlike the Western team members who breached etiquette by approaching the superiors of their Korean counterparts, the safety expert made sure to respect hierarchies in both organizations.

"Trying to resolve the issues," she told us, "the local management at the Chinese refinery would end up having conferences with our Beijing office and also with the upper management within the refinery. Eventually they understood that we weren't trying to insult them or their culture or to tell them they were bad in any way. We were trying to help. They eventually understood that there were significant fire and safety issues. But we actually had to go up some levels of management to get those resolved."

Managerial intervention to set norms early in a team's life can really help the team start out with effective processes. In one instance reported to us, a multicultural software development team's lingua franca was English, but some members, though they spoke grammatically correct English, had a very pronounced accent. In setting the ground rules for the team, the manager addressed the challenge directly, telling the members that they had been chosen for their task expertise, not their fluency in English, and that the team was going to have to work around language problems. As the project moved to the customer-services training stage, the manager advised the team members to acknowledge their accents up front. She said they should tell customers, "I realize I have an accent. If you don't understand what I'm saying, just stop me and ask questions."

One team manager addressed the language challenge directly, telling the members that they had been chosen for their task expertise, not their fluency in English, and that the team would have to work around problems.

Exit. Possibly because many of the teams we studied were project based, we found that leaving the team was an infrequent strategy for managing challenges. In short-term situations, unhappy team members often just waited out the project. When teams were permanent, producing products or services, the exit of one or more members was a strategy of last resort, but it was used—either voluntarily or after a formal request from management. Exit was likely when emotions were running high and too much face had been lost on both sides to salvage the situation.

An American member of a multicultural consulting team described the conflict between two senior consultants, one a Greek woman and the other a Polish man, over how to approach problems: "The woman from Greece would say, 'Here's the way I think we should do it.' It would be something that she was in control of. The guy from Poland would say, 'I think we should actually do it this way instead.' The woman would kind of turn red in the face, upset, and say, 'I just don't think that's the right way of doing it.' It would definitely switch from just professional differences to personal differences.

"The woman from Greece ended up leaving the firm. That was a direct result of probably all the different issues going on between these people. It really just wasn't a good fit. I've found that oftentimes when you're in consulting, you have to adapt to the culture, obviously, but you have to adapt just as much to the style of whoever is leading the project."

Though multicultural teams face challenges that are not directly attributable to cultural differences, such differences underlay whatever problem needed to be addressed in many of the teams we studied. Furthermore, while serious in their own right when they have a negative effect on team functioning, cultural challenges may also unmask fundamental managerial problems. Managers who intervene early and set norms; teams and managers who structure social interaction and work to engage everyone on the team; and teams that can see problems as stemming from culture, not personality, approach challenges with good humor and creativity. Managers who have to intervene when the team has reached a stalemate may be able to get the team moving again, but they seldom empower it to help itself the next time a stalemate occurs.

When frustrated team members take some time to think through challenges and possible solutions themselves, it can make a huge difference. Take, for example, this story about a financial-services call center. The members of the call-center team were all fluent Spanish-speakers, but some were North Americans and some were Latin Americans. Team performance, measured by calls answered per hour, was lagging. One Latin American was taking twice as long with her calls as the rest of the team. She was handling callers' questions appropriately, but she was also engaging in chitchat. When her teammates confronted her for being a free rider (they resented having to make up for her low call rate), she immediately acknowledged the problem, admitting that she did not know how to end the call politely—chitchat being normal in her culture. They rallied to help her: Using their technology, they would break into any of her calls that went overtime, excusing themselves to the customer, offering to take over the call, and saying that this employee was urgently needed to help out on a different call. The team's solution worked in the short run, and the employee got better at ending her calls in the long run.

In another case, the Indian manager of a multicultural team coordinating a companywide IT project found himself frustrated when he and a teammate from Singapore met with two Japanese members of the coordinating team to try to get the Japan section to deliver its part of the project. The Japanese members seemed to be saying yes, but in the Indian manager's view, their follow-through was insufficient. He considered and rejected the idea of going up the hierarchy to the Japanese team members' boss, and decided instead to try to build consensus with the whole Japanese IT team, not just the two members on the coordinating team. He and his Singapore teammate put together an eBusiness road show, took it to Japan, invited the whole IT team to view it at a lunch meeting, and walked through success stories about other parts of the organization that had aligned with the company's larger business priorities. It was rather subtle, he told us, but it worked. The Japanese IT team wanted to be spotlighted in future eBusiness road shows. In the end, the whole team worked well together and no higher-level manager had to get involved.

CHAPTER 9

Connect, Then Lead

In puzzling over whether it's better to be feared or loved as a leader, Machiavelli famously said that, because it's nigh impossible to do both, leaders should opt for fear. Research from Harvard Business School's Amy Cuddy and consultants Matthew Kohut and John Neffinger refutes that theory, arguing that leaders would do much better to begin with "love"—that is, to establish trust through warmth and understanding.

Most leaders today approach their jobs by emphasizing competence, strength, and credentials. But without first building a foundation of trust, they run the risk of eliciting fear, resentment, or envy.

Beginning with warmth allows trust to develop, facilitating both the exchange and the acceptance of ideas—people really hear your message and become open to it. Cultivating warmth and trust also boosts the quantity and quality of novel ideas that are produced.

The best way to gain influence is to combine warmth and strength as difficult as Machiavelli says that may be to do. In this article, the authors look at research from behavioral economics, social psychology, and other disciplines and offer practical tactics for leaders hoping to project a healthy amount of both qualities.

Is it better to be loved or feared? Niccolò Machiavelli pondered that timeless conundrum 500 years ago and hedged his bets. "It may be answered that one should wish to be both," he acknowledged, "but because it is difficult to unite them in one person, it is much safer to be feared than loved."

Now behavioral science is weighing in with research showing that Machiavelli had it partly right: When we judge others—especially our leaders—we look first at two characteristics: how lovable they are (their warmth, communion, or trustworthiness) and how fearsome they are (their strength, agency, or competence). Although there is some disagreement about the proper labels for the traits, researchers agree that they are the two primary dimensions of social judgment.

Why are these traits so important? Because they answer two critical questions: "What are this person's intentions toward me?" and "Is he or she capable of acting on those intentions?" Together, these assessments underlie our emotional and behavioral reactions to other people, groups, and even brands and companies. Research by one of us, Amy Cuddy, and colleagues Susan Fiske, of Princeton, and Peter Glick, of Lawrence University, shows that people judged to be competent but lacking in warmth often elicit envy in others, an emotion involving both respect and resentment that cuts both ways. When we respect someone, we want to cooperate or affiliate ourselves with him or her, but resentment can make that person vulnerable to harsh reprisal (think of disgraced Tyco CEO Dennis Kozlowski, whose extravagance made him an unsympathetic public figure). On the other hand, people judged as warm but incompetent tend to elicit pity, which also involves a mix of emotions: Compassion moves us to help those we pity, but our lack of respect leads us ultimately to neglect them (think of workers who become marginalized as they near retirement or of an employee with outmoded skills in a rapidly evolving industry).

To be sure, we notice plenty of other traits in people, but they're nowhere near as influential as warmth and strength. Indeed, insights from the field of psychology show that these two dimensions account for more than 90% of the variance in our positive or negative impressions we form of the people around us.

So which is better, being lovable or being strong? Most leaders today tend to emphasize their strength, competence, and credentials in the workplace, but that is exactly the wrong approach. Leaders who project strength before establishing trust run the risk of eliciting fear, and along with it a host of dysfunctional behaviors. Fear can undermine cognitive potential, creativity, and problem solving, and cause employees to get stuck and even disengage. It's a "hot" emotion, with long-lasting effects. It burns into our memory in a way that cooler emotions don't. Research by Jack Zenger and Joseph Folkman drives this point home: In a study of 51,836 leaders, only 27 of them were rated in the bottom quartile in terms of likability and in the top quartile in terms of overall leadership effectiveness—in other words, the chances that a manager who is strongly disliked will be considered a good leader are only about one in 2,000.

A growing body of research suggests that the way to influence—and to lead—is to begin with warmth. Warmth is the conduit of influence: It facilitates trust and the communication and absorption of ideas. Even a few small nonverbal signals—a nod, a smile, an open gesture—can show people that you're pleased to be in their company and attentive to their concerns. Prioritizing warmth helps you connect immediately with those around you, demonstrating that you hear them, understand them, and can be trusted by them.

When Strength Comes First

Most of us work hard to demonstrate our competence. We want to see ourselves as strong—and want others to see us the same way. We focus on warding off challenges to our strength and providing abundant evidence of competence. We feel compelled to demonstrate that we're up to the job, by striving to present the most innovative ideas in meetings, being the first to tackle a challenge, and working the longest hours. We're sure of our own intentions and thus don't feel the need to prove that we're trustworthy—despite the fact that evidence of trustworthiness is the first thing we look for in others.

Organizational psychologists Andrea Abele, of the University of Erlangen-Nuremberg, and Bogdan Wojciszke, of the University of Gdańsk, have documented this phenomenon across a variety of settings. In one experiment, when asked to choose between training programs focusing on competence-related skills (such as time management) and warmth-related ones (providing social support, for instance), most participants opted for competence-based training for themselves but soft-skills training for others. In another experiment, in which participants were asked to describe an event that shaped their self-image, most told stories about themselves that emphasized their own competence and self-determination ("I passed my pilot's license test on the first try"), whereas when they described a similar event for someone else, they focused on that person's warmth and generosity ("My friend tutored his neighbor's child in math and refused to accept any payment").

How Will People React to Your Style?

Research by Amy Cuddy, Susan Fiske, and Peter Glick suggests that the way others perceive your levels of warmth and competence determines the emotions you'll elicit and your ability to influence a situation. For example, if you're highly competent but show only moderate warmth, you'll get people to go along with you, but you won't earn their true engagement and support. And if you show no warmth, beware of those who may try to derail your efforts and maybe your career.

But putting competence first undermines leadership: Without a foundation of trust, people in the organization may comply outwardly with a leader's wishes, but they're much less likely to conform privately to adopt the values, culture, and mission of the organization in a sincere, lasting way. Workplaces lacking in trust often have a culture of "every employee for himself," in which people feel that they must be vigilant about protecting their interests. Employees can become reluctant to help others because they're unsure of whether their efforts will be reciprocated or recognized. The result: Shared organizational resources fall victim to the tragedy of the commons.

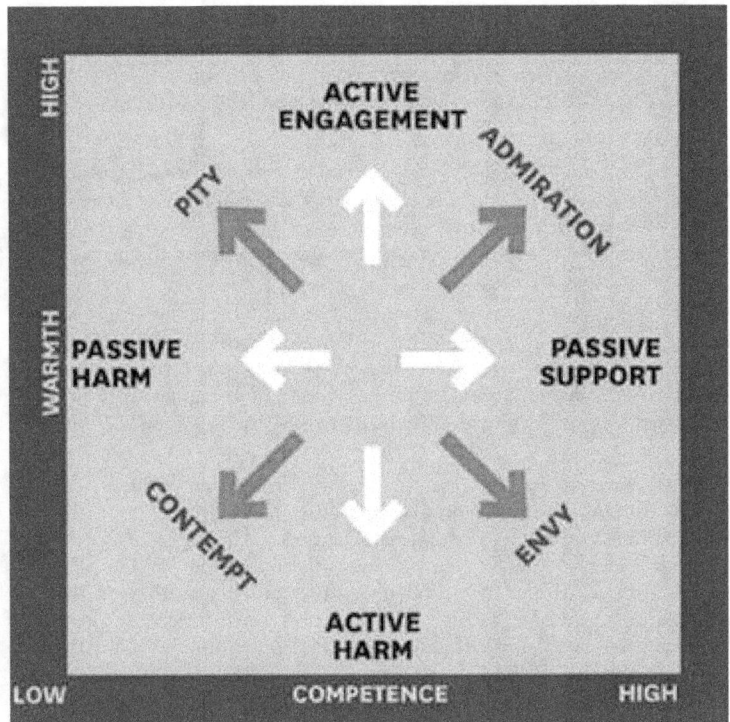

When Warmth Comes First

Although most of us strive to demonstrate our strength, warmth contributes significantly more to others' evaluations of us—and it's judged before competence. Princeton social psychologist Alex Todorov and colleagues study the cognitive and neural mechanisms that drive our "spontaneous trait inferences"—the snap judgments we make when briefly looking at faces. Their research shows that when making those judgments, people consistently pick up on warmth faster than on competence. This preference for warmth holds true in other areas as well. In a study led by Oscar Ybarra, of the University of Michigan, participants playing a word game identified warmth-related words (such as "friendly") significantly faster than competence-related ones (such as "skillful").

Why Warmth Trumps Strength

The primacy of warmth manifests in many interrelated ways that powerfully underscore the importance of connecting with people before trying to lead them.

The Need to Affiliate

People have a need to be included, to feel a sense of belonging. In fact, some psychologists would argue that the drive to affiliate ranks among our primary needs as humans. Experiments by neuroscientist Naomi Eisenberger and colleagues suggest that the need is so strong that when we are ostracized—even by virtual strangers—we experience pain that is akin to strong physical pain.

"Us" Versus "Them"

In recent decades, few areas have received as much attention from social psychology researchers as group dynamics—and for good reason: The preference for the groups to which one belongs is so strong that even under extreme conditions—such as knowing that membership in a group was randomly assigned and that the groups themselves are arbitrary—people consistently prefer fellow group members to nonmembers. As a leader, you must make sure you're a part of the key groups in your organization. In fact, you want to be the aspirational member of the group, the chosen representative of the group. As soon as you become one of "them"—the management, the leadership—you begin to lose people.

The Desire to Be Understood

People deeply desire to be heard and seen. Sadly, as important as perspective-taking is to good leadership, being in a position of power decreases people's understanding of others' points of view. When we have power over others, our ability to see them as individuals diminishes. So leaders need to consciously and consistently make the effort to imagine walking in the shoes of the people they are leading.

Behavioral economists, for their part, have shown that judgments of trustworthiness generally lead to significantly higher economic gains. For example, Mascha van 't Wout, of Brown University, and Alan Sanfey, of the University of Arizona, asked subjects to determine how an endowment should be allocated. Players invested more money, with no guarantee of return, in partners whom they perceived to be more trustworthy on the basis of a glance at their faces.

In management settings, trust increases information sharing, openness, fluidity, and cooperation. If coworkers can be trusted to do the right thing and live up to their commitments, planning, coordination, and execution are much easier. Trust also facilitates the exchange and acceptance of ideas—it allows people to hear others' message—and boosts the quantity and quality of the ideas that are produced within an organization. Most important, trust provides the opportunity to change people's attitudes and beliefs, not just their outward behavior. That's the sweet spot when it comes to influence and the ability to get people to fully accept your message.

The Happy Warrior

The best way to gain influence is to combine warmth and strength as difficult as Machiavelli says that may be to do. The traits can actually be mutually reinforcing: Feeling a sense of personal strength helps us to be more open, less threatened, and less threatening in stressful situations. When we feel confident and calm, we project authenticity and warmth.

Understanding a little bit about our chemical makeup can shed some light on how this works. The neuropeptides oxytocin and arginine vasopressin, for instance, have been linked to our ability to form human attachments, to feel and express warmth, and to behave altruistically. Recent research also suggests that across the animal kingdom feelings of strength and power have close ties to two hormones: testosterone (associated with assertiveness, reduced fear, and willingness to compete and take risks) and cortisol (associated with stress and stress reactivity).

One study, by Jennifer Lerner, Gary Sherman, Amy Cuddy, and colleagues, brought hundreds of people participating in Harvard executive-education programs into the lab and compared their levels of cortisol with the average levels of the general population. The leaders reported less stress and anxiety than did the general population, and their physiology backed that up: Their cortisol levels were significantly lower. Moreover, the higher their rank and the more subordinates they managed, the lower their cortisol level. Why? Most likely because the leaders had a heightened sense of control—a psychological factor known to have a powerful stress-buffering effect. According to research by Pranjal Mehta, of the University of Oregon, and Robert Josephs, of the University of Texas, the most effective leaders, regardless of gender, have a unique physiological profile, with relatively high testosterone and relatively low cortisol.

Such leaders face troubles without being troubled. Their behavior is not relaxed, but they are relaxed emotionally. They're often viewed as "happy warriors," and the effect of their demeanor on those around them is compelling. Happy warriors reassure us that whatever challenges we may face, things will work out in the end. Ann Richards, the former governor of Texas, played the happy warrior by pairing her assertiveness and authority with a big smile and a quick wit that made it clear she did not let the rough-and-tumble of politics get her down.

During crises, these are the people who are able to keep that influence conduit open and may even expand it. Most people hate uncertainty, but they tolerate it much better when they can look to a leader who they believe has their back and is calm, clearheaded, and courageous. These are the people we trust. These are the people we listen to.

Before people decide what they think of your message, they decide what they think of *you*.

There are physical exercises that can help to summon self-confidence and even alter your body's chemistry to be more like that of a happy warrior. Dana Carney, Amy Cuddy, and Andy Yap suggest that people adopt "power poses" associated with dominance and strength across the animal kingdom. These postures are open, expansive, and space-occupying (imagine Wonder Woman and Superman standing tall with their hands on their hips and feet spread apart). By adopting these postures for just two minutes prior to social encounters, their research shows, participants significantly increased their testosterone and decreased their cortisol levels.

Bear in mind that the signals we send can be ambiguous—we can see someone's reaction to our presence, but we may not be sure exactly what the person is reacting to. We may feel a leader's warmth but remain unsure whether it is directed at us; we sense her strength but need reassurance that it is squarely aimed at the shared challenge we face. And, as we noted earlier, judgments are often made quickly, on the basis of nonverbal cues. Especially when facing a high-pressure situation, it is useful for leaders to go through a brief warm-up routine beforehand to get in the right state of mind, practicing and adopting an attitude that will help them project positive nonverbal signals. We refer to this approach as "inside-out," in contrast to the "outside-in" strategy of trying to consciously execute specific nonverbal behaviors in the moment. Think of the difference between method acting and classical acting: In method acting, the actor experiences the emotions of the character and naturally produces an authentic performance, whereas in classical acting, actors learn to exercise precise control of their nonverbal signals. Generally speaking, an inside-out approach is more effective.

There are many tactics for projecting warmth and competence, and these can be dialed up or down as needed. Two of us, John Neffinger and Matt Kohut, work with leaders from many walks of life in mastering both nonverbal and verbal cues. Let's look now at some best practices.

How to Project Warmth

Efforts to appear warm and trustworthy by consciously controlling your nonverbal signals can backfire: All too often, you'll come off as wooden and inauthentic instead. Here are ways to avoid that trap.

Are You Projecting Warmth?

How you present yourself in workplace settings matters a great deal to how you're perceived by others. Even if you're not feeling particularly warm, practicing these approaches and using them in formal and informal situations can help clear your path to influence.

Formal Situation

Warm

- When standing, balance your weight primarily on one hip to avoid appearing rigid or tense.

- Tilt your head slightly and keep your hands open and welcoming.

Cold

- Avoid standing with your chin pointed down.
- Don't pivot your body away from the person you're engaging with.
- Avoid closed-hand positions and cutting motions.

Informal Situation

Warm

- Lean inward in a nonaggressive manner to signal interest and engagement.
- Place your hands comfortably on your knees or rest them on the table.
- Aim for body language that feels professional but relaxed.

Cold

- Try not to angle your body away from the person you're engaging.
- Crossing your arms indicates coldness and a lack of receptivity.
- Avoid sitting "at attention" or in an aggressive posture.

Find the right level.

When people want to project warmth, they sometimes amp up the enthusiasm in their voice, increasing their volume and dynamic range to convey delight. That can be effective in the right setting, but if those around you have done nothing in particular to earn your adulation, they'll assume either that you're faking it or that you fawn over everyone indiscriminately.

A better way to create vocal warmth is to speak with lower pitch and volume, as you would if you were comforting a friend. Aim for a tone that suggests that you're leveling with people—that you're sharing the straight scoop, with no pretense or emotional adornment. In doing so, you signal that you trust those you're talking with to handle things the right way. You might even occasionally share a personal story—one that feels private but not inappropriate—in a confiding tone of voice to demonstrate that you're being forthcoming and open. Suppose, for instance, that you want to establish a bond with new employees you're meeting for the first time. You might offer something personal right off the bat, such as recalling how you felt at a similar point in your career. That's often enough to set a congenial tone.

Validate feelings.

Before people decide what they think of your message, they decide what they think of *you*. If you show your employees that you hold roughly the same worldview they do, you demonstrate not only empathy but, in their eyes, common sense—the ultimate qualification for being listened to. So if you want colleagues to listen and agree with you, first agree with them.

Imagine, for instance, that your company is undergoing a major reorganization and your group is feeling deep anxiety over what the change could mean—for quality, innovation, job security. Acknowledge people's fear and concerns when you speak to them, whether in formal meetings or during watercooler chats. Look them in the eye and say, "I know everybody's feeling a lot of uncertainty right now, and it's unsettling." People will respect you for addressing the elephant in the room, and will be more open to hearing what you have to say.

Smile—and mean it.

When we smile sincerely, the warmth becomes self-reinforcing: Feeling happy makes us smile, and smiling makes us happy. This facial feedback is also contagious. We tend to mirror one another's nonverbal expressions and emotions, so when we see someone beaming and emanating genuine warmth, we can't resist smiling ourselves.

Warmth is not easy to fake, of course, and a polite smile fools no one. To project warmth, you have to genuinely feel it. A natural smile, for instance, involves not only the muscles around the mouth but also those around the eyes—the crow's feet.

So how do you produce a natural smile? Find some reason to feel happy wherever you may be, even if you have to resort to laughing at your predicament. Introverts in social settings can single out one person to focus on. This can help you channel the sense of comfort you feel with close friends or family.

For example, KNP worked with a manager who was having trouble connecting with her employees. Having come up through the ranks as a highly analytic engineer, she projected competence and determination, but not much warmth. We noticed, however, that when she talked about where she grew up and what she learned about life from the tight-knit community in her neighborhood, her demeanor relaxed and she smiled broadly. By including a brief anecdote about her upbringing when she kicked off a meeting or made a presentation, she was able to show her colleagues a warm and relatable side of herself.

One thing to avoid: smiling with your eyebrows raised at anyone over the age of five. This suggests that you are overly eager to please and be liked. It also signals anxiety, which, like warmth, is contagious. It will cost you much more in strength than you will gain in warmth.

How to Project Strength

Strength or competence can be established by virtue of the position you hold, your reputation, and your actual performance. But your presence, or demeanor, always counts, too. The way you carry yourself doesn't establish your skill level, of course, but it is taken as strong evidence of your attitude—how serious you are and how determined to tackle a challenge—and that is an important component of overall strength. The trick is to cultivate a demeanor of strength without seeming menacing.

Feel in command.

Warmth may be harder to fake, but confidence is harder to talk yourself into. Feeling like an impostor—that you don't belong in the position you're in and are going to be "found out"—is very common. But self-doubt completely undermines your ability to project confidence, enthusiasm, and passion, the qualities that make up presence. In fact, if you see yourself as an impostor, others will, too. Feeling in command and confident is about connecting with yourself. And when we are connected with ourselves, it is much easier to connect with others.

Holding your body in certain ways, as we discussed previously, can help. Although we refer to these postures as power poses, they don't increase your dominance over others. They're about personal power—your agency and ability to self-regulate. Recent research led by Dacher Keltner, of the University of California, Berkeley, shows that feeling powerful in this way allows you to shed the fears and inhibitions that can prevent you from bringing your fullest, most authentic and enthusiastic self to a high-stakes professional situation, such as a pitch to investors or a speech to an influential audience.

Stand up straight.

It is hard to overstate the importance of good posture in projecting authority and an intention to be taken seriously. As Maya Angelou wrote, "Stand up straight and realize who you are, that you tower over your circumstances." Good posture does not mean the exaggerated chest-out pose known in the military as standing at attention, or raising one's chin up high. It just means reaching your full height, using your muscles to straighten the S-curve in your spine rather than slouching. It sounds trivial, but maximizing the physical space your body takes up makes a substantial difference in how your audience reacts to you, regardless of your height.

Get ahold of yourself.

When you move, move deliberately and precisely to a specific spot rather than casting your limbs about loose-jointedly. And when you are finished moving, be still. Twitching, fidgeting, or other visual static sends the signal that you're not in control. Stillness demonstrates calm. Combine that with good posture, and you'll achieve what's known as poise, which telegraphs equilibrium and stability, important aspects of credible leadership presence.

Standing tall is an especially good way to project strength because it doesn't interfere with warmth in the way that other signals of strength—cutting gestures, a furrowed brow, an elevated chin—often do. People who instruct their children to stand up straight and smile are on to something: This simple combination is perhaps the best way to project strength and warmth simultaneously.If you want to effectively lead others, you have to get the warmth-competence dynamic right. Projecting both traits at once is difficult, but the two can be mutually reinforcing—and the rewards substantial. Earning the trust and appreciation of those around you feels good. Feeling in command of a situation does, too. Doing both lets you influence people more effectively.

The strategies we suggest may seem awkward at first, but they will soon create a positive feedback loop. Being calm and confident creates space to be warm, open, and appreciative, to choose to act in ways that reflect and express your values and priorities. Once you establish your warmth, your strength is received as a welcome reassurance. Your leadership becomes not a threat but a gift.

CHAPTER 10
Getting Virtual Teams Right

With more and more companies doing business in far-flung places and more and more employees telecommuting, virtual teams—those made up of people in different physical locations—are on the rise. Geographic separation can make it challenging for dispersed teammates to communicate and collaborate. But evidence suggests that if virtual work groups are well managed, they can outperform teams with common office space.

Consultants at Ferrazzi Greenlight believe that four elements are crucial for success:

The right team. Start by assembling qualified people who can work independently and flexibly. Keep the group size small, and divide the labor appropriately.

- *The right leadership.*Effective managers foster trust, encourage open dialogue, and set clear goals and guidelines.

- *The right touchpoints.* Virtual teammates should meet face-to-face occasionally. This is especially useful when a project kicks off, when someone new comes on board, and when key milestones or problems occur.

- *The right technology.* To maximize productivity, install easy-to-use systems for conference calling, making direct calls, sending text messages, and participating in online discussion forums and virtual team rooms.

"Virtual" teams—ones made up of people in different physical locations—are on the rise. As companies expand geographically and as telecommuting becomes more common, work groups often span far-flung offices, shared workspaces, private homes, and hotel rooms. When my firm, Ferrazzi Greenlight, recently surveyed 1,700 knowledge workers, 79% reported working always or frequently in dispersed teams. Armed with laptops, Wi-Fi, and mobile phones, most professionals can do their jobs from anywhere.

The appeal of forming virtual teams is clear. Employees can manage their work and personal lives more flexibly, and they have the opportunity to interact with colleagues around the world. Companies can use the best and lowest-cost global talent and significantly reduce their real estate costs.

But virtual teams are hard to get right. In their seminal 2001 study of 70 such groups, professors Vijay Govindarajan and Anil Gupta found that 82% fell short of their goals and 33% rated themselves as largely unsuccessful. A 2005 Deloitte study of IT projects outsourced to virtual work groups found that 66% failed to satisfy the clients' requirements. And in our research, we've discovered that most people consider virtual communication less productive than face-to-face interaction, and nearly half admit to feeling confused and overwhelmed by collaboration technology.

There is good news, however. A 2009 study of 80 global software teams by authors from BCG and WHU-Otto Beisheim School of Management indicates that well-managed dispersed teams can actually outperform those that share office space. Similarly, an Aon Consulting report noted that using virtual teams can improve employee productivity; some organizations have seen gains of up to 43%.

So how do you create and lead an effective virtual team? There's a lot of advice out there, but through our research and our experience helping organizations navigate collaboration challenges, we've concluded that there are four must-haves: the right team, the right leadership, the right touchpoints, and the right technology. By following simple high-return practices for each, managers can maximize the productivity of teams they must lead virtually.

The Right Team

Team composition should be your starting point. You won't get anywhere without hiring (or developing) people suited to virtual teamwork, putting them into groups of the right size, and dividing the labor appropriately.

People.

We've found that successful virtual team players all have a few things in common: good communication skills, high emotional intelligence, an ability to work independently, and the resilience to recover from the snafus that inevitably arise. Awareness of and sensitivity to other cultures is also important in global groups. When building a team, leaders should conduct behavioral interviews and personality tests like the Myers-Briggs to screen for all those qualities. If you inherit a team, use the same tools to take stock of your people and assess their weaknesses; then train them in the skills they're lacking, encourage them to coach one another, and consider reassignment for those who don't make progress.

Size.

Teams have been getting larger and larger, sometimes even exceeding 100 people for complex projects, according to one study. But our work with companies from large multinationals to tiny start-ups has taught us that the most effective virtual teams are small ones—fewer than 10 people. OnPoint Consulting's research supports this: Of the virtual teams the firm studied, the worst performers had 13 members or more. "Social loafing" is one cause. Research shows that team members reduce effort when they feel less responsible for output. The effect kicks in when teams exceed four or five members. As groups grow, another challenge is ensuring inclusive communication. The late Harvard psychology professor Richard Hackman noted that it takes only 10 conversations for every person on a team of five to touch base with everyone else, but that number rises to 78 for a team of 13. Thus to optimize your group's performance, don't assemble too many players.

Roles.

When projects require the efforts of multiple people from various departments, we devise appropriate subteams. Our approach is similar to the X-team strategy advocated by MIT professor Deborah Ancona, who defines three tiers of team members: core, operational, and outer. The core consists of executives responsible for strategy. The operational group leads and makes decisions about day-to-day work but doesn't tackle the larger issues handled by the core. And the outer network consists of temporary or part-time members who are brought in for a particular stage of the project because of their specialized expertise.

Ferrazzi Greenlight worked with a large multinational manufacturing company to help a dispersed team make better cross-division decisions, particularly when product output from one area fed others. The group was composed of more than 30 members—a mix of HQ, operational, and divisional leaders, some of whom reported to others. While many had knowledge vital to the work at hand, a fair number were included on an honorary basis. By the time we were asked to help, teammates openly acknowledged that they were in disarray and unable to achieve their financial goals. We brought everyone together for a face-to-face summit and then broke the group into smaller constituencies to brainstorm short-term wins. Those subteams continued to meet virtually after all parties were back in their respective offices. One group, made up of five divisional GMs, latched onto the goal of greater cross-selling and had a near-immediate success story: As a small, narrowly focused team, they were able to recognize that a plentiful stabilization agent used in ice cream could be repurposed to replace a scarce agent needed by other customers, including makers of hairstyling products and fracking fluids.

The Right Leadership

A recent study of engineering groups showed that the best predictor of success for managers leading dispersed teams is experience doing it before. That said, we've seen even novices excel by practicing some key behaviors that, while also critical in face-to-face settings, must be amplified in virtual ones:

Fostering trust.

Trust starts with respect and empathy. So, early on, leaders should encourage team members to describe their backgrounds, the value they hope to add to the group, and the way they prefer to work. Another practice, utilized by Tony Hsieh and Jenn Lim at their entirely virtual organization, Delivering Happiness, is to ask new hires to give video tours of their workspaces. This allows colleagues to form mental images of one another when they're later communicating by e-mail, phone, or text message. Remember too that relationship building should be an ongoing process. While employees who are in the same office commonly chat about their lives, virtual teammates do so much more rarely. Try taking five minutes at the beginning of conference calls for everyone to share a recent professional success or some personal news. This is probably the easiest way to overcome the isolation that can creep in when people don't work together physically.

Encouraging open dialogue.

If you've established trust, you've set everyone up for open dialogue, or "observable candor"—a behavior that professors James O'Toole and the late Warren Bennis described as a foundation of successful teamwork. Our own recent study of 50 financial firms confirmed that leaders of dispersed groups, in particular, must push members to be frank with one another. One way to do this is by modeling "caring criticism." When delivering negative feedback, use phrases like "I might suggest" and "Think about this." When receiving such feedback, thank the person who offered it and confirm points of agreement. A tactic for conference calls is to designate one team member to act as the official advocate for candor—noticing and speaking up when something is being left unsaid and calling out criticism that's not constructive. On the flip side, you should also occasionally recognize people for practices that improve team communication and collaboration.

The Dangers of Distance

Geographic separation is just one challenge facing 21st-century work groups. Karen Sobel Lojeski of Stony Brook University and Richard Reilly of the Stevens Institute of Technology calculate the "virtual distance" among teammates by charting three types of distance:

- **Physical**—geographic or temporal separation, or affiliation with different departments or organizations

- **Operational**—variations in team size, the extent of members' other commitments, the amount of face-to-face interaction, or technical skills and support

- **Affinity**—differences in culture, rank, or the level of interdependence and preexisting relationships

When rating teams on a five-point scale in each subcategory, Lojeski and Reilly found that teams with high virtual-distance scores overall showed drops in:

- **Trust**—down 83%

- **Innovation**—down 93%

- **Satisfaction**—down 80%

- **Performance**—down 50%

Even colleagues on different floors in the same building might be considered physically distant, and operational and affinity distance can certainly affect colocated workers. But the associated problems are more common—and more acute—for virtual teams.

Clarifying goals and guidelines.

Management gurus from John Kotter to Chip and Dan Heath acknowledge the importance of establishing a common purpose or vision, while also framing the work in terms of team members' individual needs and ambitions. Explain to everyone why you are coming together and what benefits will result, and then keep reiterating the message.

Specific guidelines for team interaction are equally vital; research shows that rules reduce uncertainty and enhance trust in social groups, thereby improving productivity. Agree on how quickly team members should respond to queries and requests from one another, and outline follow-up steps if someone is slow to act. Virtual teammates often find themselves saying, "I thought it was obvious that…" or "I didn't think I needed to spell that out." So also insist that requests be specific. Instead of saying "Circle back to me," state whether you want to give final input on a decision or simply be informed after the decision is made. If you have a conference call about project details, follow up with an e-mail to minimize misunderstandings.

Also make it clear that multitasking on calls isn't OK. According to a recent study, 82% of people admit to doing other things—from surfing the web to using the bathroom—during team calls. But virtual collaboration requires that everyone be mentally present and engaged. Explain your policy, and when the group has a virtual meeting, regularly call on people to share their thoughts. Better yet, switch to video, which can essentially eliminate multitasking.

Delivering Happiness finds that using video also reinforces one of the company's core values: having fun. At the start of videoconference calls, participants pretend to make direct eye contact as their images appear side by side on-screen, much like the opening of the hit 1970s TV show, *The Brady Bunch*. New agenda items are often introduced with music—for example, to lead into a discussion on driving the firm's long-term growth, the emcee might play "Stayin' Alive" by the Bee Gees, causing everyone to burst into dance. The fun and camaraderie match anything coworkers experience in person while ensuring that people are engaged in the conversation and focused on the specific tasks or topics at hand.

The Right Touchpoints

Virtual teams should come together in person at certain times. Here are the stages at which it's most critical:

Kickoff.

An initial meeting, face-to-face if possible and using video if not, will go a long way toward introducing teammates, setting expectations for trust and candor, and clarifying team goals and behavioral guidelines. Eye contact and body language help to kindle personal connections and the "swift trust" that allows a group of strangers to work together before long-term bonds develop. This is when you can assess team dynamics and work to bridge specific gaps—for example, by assigning an achievable task to a pair of dissimilar colleagues, allowing them a "small win"—as HBS professor Teresa Amabile calls it—together.

Onboarding.

Too often, plans for bringing new people onto a virtual team consist of a short e-mail or conference-call introduction to the rest of the group and a dozen or more documents that the newcomers are supposed to read and digest. A much better approach is to give them the same in-person welcome you gave the group. Fly them into headquarters or another location to meet with you and others who will be important to their success. Encourage them to videoconference with the rest of their teammates. We also recommend pairing newcomers with a mentor who can answer questions quickly but personally—the equivalent of a friendly colleague with an office around the corner.

Milestones.

Virtual team leaders need to continually motivate members to deliver their best, but e-mail updates and weekly conference calls are not enough to sustain momentum. In the absence of visual cues and body language, misunderstandings often arise, especially on larger teams. Team members begin to feel disconnected and less engaged, and their contributions to the project decline. So get people together to celebrate the achievement of short-term goals or to crack tough problems.

Ritesh Idnani, founder and CEO of Seamless Health, a health care start-up that relies on dispersed teams of managers, is adamant about bringing everyone together in person at least quarterly. Also, whenever someone new joins the team, he allocates two weeks for that individual to talk to colleagues deemed "important to know," who can share information about the company and the job. "After that, I ask the person to sit down with me and tell me what he or she learned," says Idnani. Not only does the new hire gain valuable insights, but Idnani does too. "You end up learning a lot from someone coming from the outside with a fresh pair of eyes."

The Right Technology

In our experience, even top-notch virtual teams—those with the most-talented workers, the finest leadership, and frequent touchpoints—can be felled by poor technology. We recommend using platforms that integrate all types of communication and include these key components:

Conference calling.

Look for systems that don't require access codes (helpful for team members who are driving) but do record automatically or with a single click and facilitate or automate transcription. The best systems even help monitor the time that each individual spends talking versus listening. Also consider one-on-one and group videoconferencing, since visual cues help establish empathy and trust.

Direct calling and text messaging.

By supporting real-time conversation between two remote participants, direct calls are one of the simplest and most powerful tools in the arsenal. And as teenagers know, texting is a surprisingly effective way to maintain personal relationships.

Discussion forums or virtual team rooms.

Software ranging from Microsoft SharePoint to Moot allows team members to present issues to the entire group, for colleagues to study or comment on when they have time. Scholars refer to this sort of collaboration as "messy talk" and say it's critical for completing complex projects. People can even weigh in on topics outside their domain and still offer useful input; research has shown that the best solutions to problems often come from unexpected sources. All interaction is documented and therefore becomes a searchable database.

When collaboration platforms combine all the elements above, they become the center of team activities, and using them brings greater efficiency, not extra, unnecessary work.

John Stepper, a managing director at Deutsche Bank, created the bank's Communities of Practice electronic discussion forums, in which 100,000 employees now converse with colleagues in similar roles around the world. Stepper calls this collaboration "working out loud." All the activity is open and searchable, making it easy for existing teams to find subject-matter experts or review their own work and for ad hoc teams to form around business-related passions. For example, when Stepper made data on employee resource use available, a few interested parties self-organized into a virtual project team to create a system that documents individuals' cost savings over time. As people began to compete for the biggest savings, the company benefited. "What's important is that you're identifying common niches and connecting people toward some purpose," he explains.

The earliest virtual teams were formed to facilitate innovation among top experts around the world who didn't have time to travel. Today teams of physically dispersed employees are more often just a necessity of doing business. Companies can boost such groups' productivity, though—even beyond that of teams who share office space—by following the practices we describe here.

www.ingramcontent.com/pod-product-compliance
Lightning Source LLC
Chambersburg PA
CBHW070833180526
45168CB00002B/819